WATERLOO STATION

A history
of London's busiest terminus

BURROWING BENEATH WATERLOO STATION.

How the New Underground Station is Being Constructed in the "Vaults" of the Over-ground Station

THE BIG TRIPLE ESCALATOR DESCENDING TO THE NEW UNDERGROUND STATION AT WATERLOO

Very little is generally known of the important developments, with due regard to future expansion, now in full swing in several parts of London's Underground. Nor is the unsuspecting traveller aware, as he walks the subways, of the intriguing and complex growth of the burrowings which are taking place, in many cases, just below his feet. The latest of these unprecedented examples of pure modernity is at Waterloo Station, where the booking hall, escalators and subways shown are being constructed to the new platforms of the Kennington Loop, Waterloo Station itself stands upon arches, and through one of these the big triple escalator will descend, clearing either pier by only two inches, and cutting eighteen inches into the foundations. To do this the most ingenious underpinning, beside which that required at Waterloo Bridge, in the event of its repair, would be comparatively simple—and now almost complete—has been resorted to, to strengthen the foundations and sheathe the escalator tunnel. The old foundations are bedded in gravel which carries a 14 ft. depth of water. To exclude this from the workings a cofferdam of steel piling, enclosing both piers, was put down right into the underlying clay. Inside this "tank" the underpinning was variously filled as shown, resulting not only in the new accommodation, but actually a much stronger foundation than was formerly the case. At the far ends the piers were also cut right through to pass an unbroken barricade of the piling, and, in the way of the booking hall, are being entirely removed and steel stanchions substituted to support the arches. The engineer responsible for this fine, ambitious work is Mr. H. H. Dalrymple-Hay, M.Inst.C.E., to whose credit must also be placed the new Charing Cross construction we recently illustrated. The picture is shown looking towards Kennington.

Cutaway of Waterloo station Underground, 1926.

ROBERT LORDAN

WATERLOO STATION

A history
of London's busiest terminus

THE CROWOOD PRESS

First published in 2021 by
The Crowood Press Ltd
Ramsbury, Marlborough
Wiltshire SN8 2HR

enquiries@crowood.com

www.crowood.com

British Library Cataloguing-in-Publication Data
A catalogue record for this book is available from the British Library.

ISBN 978 1 78500 868 9

Front cover image 'Apocalypse Now – Waterloo Station' provided with permission
by Tim Green.

Typeset by Simon and Sons

Cover design by Sergey Tsvetkov

Printed in India by Replika Press Pvt. Ltd.

Contents

Dedication		6
Acknowledgements		6
List of Abbreviations		6
Introduction		7
Chapter 1	Early Days	8
Chapter 2	Onwards to Waterloo	21
Chapter 3	Chaos Comes to York Road	33
Chapter 4	The Necropolis Railway	53
Chapter 5	Waterloo East	70
Chapter 6	Waterloo Underground	82
Chapter 7	Transformation and World War I	99
Chapter 8	The 1920s, 1930s and World War II	120
Chapter 9	Post-War Waterloo	128
Chapter 10	Waterloo International	142
Chapter 11	Waterloo in Culture	149
Bibliography		156
Illustration Credits		156
Index		157

Dedication

For my grandmother, Josephine Tobitt.

Acknowledgements

I would like to express my gratitude to all those who have supported me in this endeavour: my parents, Rachel and Michael Lordan, my grandmother, Josephine Tobitt, Irene, Stewart and Neil, and my partner, Elaine.

Special thanks also to my family in Canada, and in the UK, my dear friends Alex and Mike, Ainslie and Doug, Melanie and Stuart, Mark and Caroline, and Chas Taylor. The positivity with which you bless me is invaluable.

A special mention must go in particular to those who have so kindly and selflessly provided me with images, information and other help along the way: Iain Wakeford, Christopher Cox, Barry Kitchener (who provided me with a fascinating tour behind Waterloo's scenes), Brandon Rumsey, Richard Galpin, Mark Crail, Steve Knight, Michael Day, Michelle Howe, Justin and Terry Foulger, Hugh Llewellyn and the Fathers of Saint Edward Monastery, Brookwood.

Thank you all.

List of Abbreviations

BEA: British European Airways
BR: British Rail
BS&WR: The Baker Street & Waterloo Railway
CC&WERC: The Charing Cross and Waterloo Electric Railway Company
CCRC: Charing Cross Railway Company
CL&RR: City of London & Richmond Railway
GJR: The Guildford Junction Railway
GLC: Greater London Council
GNLCC: Great Northern London Cemetery Company
GWR: Great Western Railway
L&GR: London & Greenwich Railway
L&SR: London & Southampton Railway
L&SWR: London & South Western Railway
LCC: London County Council
LNC: London Necropolis Company
R&WEJR: Richmond & West End Junction Railway
SER: South Eastern Railway
SW&CJR: South Western & City Junction Railway
W&WR: Waterloo & Whitehall Railway
W&CR: Waterloo & City Railway
W&RER: The Waterloo & Royal Exchange Railway
WEL&CPR: West End of London & Crystal Palace Railway
WLER: West London Extension Railway

Introduction

Music-hall star Marie Lloyd was once described by theatre critic James Agate as having 'a heart as big as Waterloo Station'. That's praise indeed, because Waterloo is enormous: covering over 24 acres (9.7ha) and with twenty-four platforms, it is the UK's largest railway terminal. It is Britain's busiest too – in 2019 alone the station handled 94.2 million journeys.

Waterloo has long been integral to the fabric of London. Along with its links to Southampton, Portsmouth and the West Country, Waterloo is a vital commuter hub, shepherding millions of commuters to and from their work in the capital. In this process it is aided by Waterloo East, a satellite station tethered to Waterloo main via a sprawling set of corridors, and its own dedicated tube line – the turquoise-coloured Waterloo & City, which shuttles workers to and from London's financial Square Mile.

For many years, when boat trains thundered to and from the mighty ocean liners at Southampton Docks, Waterloo was also a major international gateway, the first impression of London for countless overseas visitors, from tourists and American film stars, to thousands of Windrush Generation émigrés. For a brief period in the late twentieth and early twenty-first centuries, Waterloo took on a similar international role, this time as London's first Channel Tunnel terminal.

At the centre of it all is Waterloo's famous clock. Hanging high above the concourse, this landmark has witnessed much since it was installed: from war and state funerals, to royal weddings and the station's numerous cosmetic changes… not to mention many a romantic liaison.

Waterloo and the city it has served for over 170 years have endured and survived many perils and experiences, and it is my hope that those passing through Waterloo will be encouraged to pause and consider the historic significance of this building. For the history of London Waterloo is a fascinating one, full of innovation, intrigue and human interest; a story truly worthy of being told.

I therefore consider it an honour to share it with you here.

Robert Lordan, Buckinghamshire,
August 2020

Aerial view of Waterloo at night, 2011.

CHAPTER I

Early Days

Ironic as it may sound, it can be argued that the sequence of events that eventually led to the establishment of Waterloo station was initiated by the Napoleonic Wars. During that period (and indeed throughout the centuries preceding it) the swiftest route between London and strategic points on the south coast was waterborne, via the Thames and the Strait of Dover. Although Britain had secured naval dominance at the Battle of Trafalgar in 1805, the danger posed to vessels traversing the English Channel had never been more apparent, and it was clear that a more direct inland route – which would also avoid the perils of bad weather – would be hugely beneficial.

Canals Show the Way

With this in mind, moves were made to forge a canal linking London and the nation's naval powerhouse, Portsmouth. Only two short sections of this grand vision came to fruition: the Wey & Arun Canal, which runs from Pallingham in West Sussex to Shalford, just south of Guildford; and the Portsmouth & Arundel Canal, a now filled-in waterway that cut across Portsea Island. Both of these networks missed out on serving their original purpose, having been completed shortly after Napoleon's defeat at the Battle of Waterloo in 1815.

Map of Portsea Canal, 1815.

However, although the conflict with France was over, the idea of connecting the capital to Portsmouth via an inland course had taken hold, and a little further west along the coast, business leaders in Southampton were watching with a keen eye. Realizing the trade benefits that such a link would bring, they too began to plan for a similar canal, although it was soon realized that such a project would be far too costly.

Fortunately, a new and exciting mode of transport was beginning to make itself known in the north of England, demonstrated by the Stockton & Darlington Railway that opened in 1825, and the Liverpool & Manchester Railway that followed in 1830.

A Railway for London and Southampton

Quick to spot the potential of railway travel, a group of three men – all of whom had garnered a grim knowledge of business and shipping through their involvement with the slave trade – gathered on 6 October 1830 to draft a prospectus for a railway line connecting Southampton and London. This trio were politician and former army officer, Abel Rous Dottin (whose

Abel Rous Dottin.

Southampton home, Bugle Hall, provided the venue for the meeting), Robert Johnston (who would later participate in the planning of the London & Greenwich Railway – the L&GW) and American-born Robert Shedden Jr.

In the early nineteenth century Southampton was a minor port. To give an idea of how some perceived the town at the time, we have this rather unflattering description from a history of the railway, published in the late Victorian era:

> *As for Southampton, it boasted a population of only 19,000; its shipping accommodation was of the poorest description; unsightly mud banks surrounded the town, and shipmasters were often heard to declare that instead of being called upon to pay port dues, they themselves should be paid for coming thither.*

Due to these poor facilities, Dottin, Johnston and Shedden considered it would be advantageous to construct a modern network of docks and warehouses in Southampton as a means of encouraging freight for their prospective railway. To boost trade further, it was also anticipated that a branch line would be built, connecting Southampton to Bath and Bristol via Basingstoke.

These facets came together to create the company's rather ponderous name, 'The Southampton, London & Branch Railway & Dock Company', which was formed in 1831. Clumsy title aside, the proposal proved popular. One newspaper at the time reported that:

> *The projected Railway from Southampton to London is a subject which now appears to occupy the attention of every class of society in this town [Southampton] and along the whole of the intended line of road…our neighbours in France are alive to the subject, and several agents are arrived to obtain information.*

Further support came when the company held its first public meeting at The London Tavern, Bishopsgate, at midday on 1 December 1831.

The London Tavern

Despite sounding like a quaint pub, The London Tavern was in fact a grand banqueting hall where many important business gatherings were held. It was especially popular with burgeoning railway companies during the early nineteenth century. The establishment was noted for its turtle soup, and the cellar contained large water tanks in which the unfortunate creatures were kept. As we shall later see, Waterloo station played a major role in supplying London with this now taboo delicacy.

The London Tavern.

However, problems with the scheme soon began to appear. The dock construction aspect was deemed too expensive, whilst the Basingstoke branch brought the company into conflict with the Great Western Railway (GWR), who also had their sights set on Bristol.

It was decided therefore to shed these two elements and strip the project down to a straightforward connection between London and Southampton. This allowed for a much sharper name, 'The London & Southampton Railway Company' (L&SR), which was adopted in 1834 – and on 25 July of that same year, a parliamentary bill granted the enterprise royal assent.

Construction

Having raised a budget of one million pounds, construction of the L&SR commenced in autumn 1834 under the direction of engineer Francis Giles. A protégé of John Rennie, Giles was already well acquainted with the route, having surveyed it during the period when it was envisioned as a canal.

A cautious and conscientious man, Giles was noted for a dispute he had engaged in with that other great railway engineer, George Stephenson, which had occurred during a committee examining the planning stages of the Liverpool & Manchester Railway. Giles had opposed the scheme, and noting that Stephenson intended to take the line across the boggy expanse of Chat Moss, declared that 'no engineer in his senses would go through Chat Moss if he wanted to make a railroad from Liverpool to Manchester.'

Stephenson, of course, succeeded in proving this rather scathing remark wrong, and when it came to scrutinizing the route of the London to Southampton line, he had the opportunity to get his own back.

When the bill was being discussed in parliament, Stephenson's expertise was called upon, giving him the opportunity to throw Giles' words back at him in what was no doubt a satisfying retort: 'No engineer in his senses would go through Basingstoke if he wanted to make a railway from London to Southampton.' Stephenson twisted the knife further, predicting 'the whole wealth of the company would be forever buried in the St George's Hill cutting at Weybridge.'

Although he, too, was wrong about his opponent's engineering knowhow, Stephenson was partially correct with regard to the project's finances. Construction proved slow, and after two years Giles found himself well over his original budget, forcing him to increase the figure from £894,874 to £1,507,753 – over £197 million in today's money.

Joseph Locke

Born in Attercliffe, Sheffield, in 1805, Joseph Locke first trained to be a mining engineer, a role that would put him in good stead for his career as a master railway builder. At the age of eighteen he began to study under George Stephenson, and had a part in the construction of the Liverpool & Manchester Railway. After this he moved on to survey the Grand Junction Railway between Birmingham and Warrington.

So impressed were they with his work that the GJR directors hinted that Locke should take sole responsibility for the project; this suggestion greatly upset Stephenson. As well as lines in England, Locke also constructed railways in Scotland, France, Spain and Holland. He died in 1860.

Joseph Locke.

Despite the project being in southern England, many of the shareholders hailed from Lancashire, and upon hearing of Giles' revised estimate, these rather blunt fellows had him dismissed. They replaced Giles with Joseph Locke, who, in a meeting of shareholders at The London Tavern on 31 August 1837, provided a summary of the changes and savings he'd made. These included employing fellow railway engineer, Thomas Brassey – whom Locke described as a 'very able and responsible contractor' – to 'execute all the remaining works from Wandsworth to the River Wey', and by making contractors south of the Wey responsible for sourcing their own building materials.

Locke also suggested the line be opened in sections so a profit could be turned whilst other parts of the route were being finalized. This approach was adopted, thus enabling the first stretch – between Nine Elms (near Vauxhall) and Woking Common – to open for service in May 1838, precisely in accordance with Locke's revised schedule.

Early Test Runs

In the weeks leading up to the official opening of the L&SR's first section, a number of private trial runs were held, the first of which took place on Saturday 28 April 1838. The weather that day was perfect and spirits were high as Joseph Locke, along with the project's directors, members of parliament and several noblemen, boarded carriages at Nine Elms – the L&SR's first London terminus.

As the train chugged down to Woking Common, the fine weather allowed the VIP passengers a delightful view of the passing countryside, and many spectators gathered along the 23 miles (37km) of track to witness the historic event. The service reached Woking Common in forty-five minutes and managed the return journey to Nine Elms in forty-three.

On Saturday 26 May – two days before the L&SR's official opening – another set of private runs took place, to which some 200 friends and family of the directors and shareholders were invited. When reporting on this excursion, *The Manchester*

Guardian described the first-class carriages in considerable detail:

> The carriages are so arranged as to accommodate 18 persons, being divided into three compartments, each capable of containing six passengers. Of these, those that are denominated 'first class' conveyances are elegantly and tastefully fitted up, somewhat in the form of stalls or high-sided armchairs, with cushions and linings in drab-cloth.
>
> Indeed, they are so extremely comfortable and roomy, notwithstanding six passengers are assigned to one compartment, that we are confident there are many persons who will think the time occupied in the transit from place to place far too short.

Although the day was deemed a success, there was one minor incident in which a 'trifling accident to one of the valves' occurred on one of the engines. This resulted in a loss of water, causing the service to grind to a halt at Ditton Marsh station. The engine was swiftly hauled to Hersham Green for a quick top-up, a process that took twenty minutes.

As it reversed back into Ditton Marsh, however, another train – this one hauled by an engine named the *Tartar*, which was under the control of Joseph Locke – puffed into view in the opposing direction, a spectacle that caused some minor panic. According to one report, a number of passengers on the stranded train hastily abandoned the carriages, fearing that a collision was imminent. Thankfully the situation was under control, and Locke calmly urged the guests to return to their seats.

The Nine Elms to Woking section finally opened to the public on Monday 21 May 1838, with five passenger services in each direction per day. To provide this date with some context, Charles Dickens was still in the middle of serializing *Oliver Twist*, Liszt, Mendelssohn and Berlioz were providing the music of the day, and Queen Victoria – whose coronation would be held the following month – had only just turned nineteen.

L&SR timetable, 1838.

Nine Elms Terminus

The precursor to Waterloo station was the L&SR's first terminal at Nine Elms, an area beside the River Thames, sandwiched between Battersea and Vauxhall. Today, Nine Elms is a rather soulless place, having undergone a recent boom in construction, which has resulted in a cluster of metallic glass towers. These are accompanied by the new American Embassy, a squat, cube-like fortress perched in the middle of a moat.

In the 1830s, however, Nine Elms was decidedly pastoral, described at the time as being 'low and marshy, studded with windmills and pollard trees and Dutch-like in appearance.' Another contemporary account from *The South Western, or London, Southampton, and Portsmouth Railway Guide*, described the area thus:

Nine Elms site in 2020.

Nine Elms is partly occupied by villas and partly by garden-ground and wharfs. Here are perhaps some of the nearest corn-fields in the metropolitan district. A large brook passes through it from under the railroad, and on falling into the Thames, turns a tide-mill.

LONDON AND SOUTHAMPTON RAILWAY—LONDON STATION.

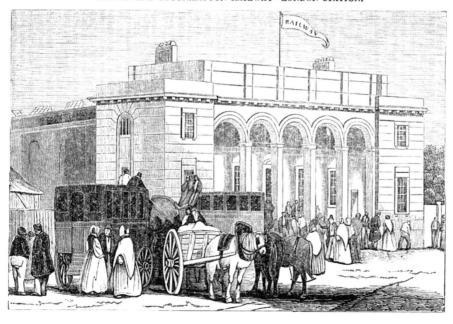

Nine Elms terminal, 1838.

What's in a Name?

Despite sounding literal, the precise origin of the term 'Nine Elms' is somewhat vague. The first distinct reference dates from the mid-1640s, in which a farm and brewery of the same name are mentioned. 'Vauxhall', meanwhile, is a corruption of 'Falke's Hall', a large house that once stood in the area and was named after its owner, Falkes de Breauté, an Anglo-Norman soldier from the early thirteenth century who was loyal to King John.

In a curious historical twist, the Russian term for station – 'вокзал' – is pronounced 'Vokzal' and is said to have been inspired by the area, although this was apparently more of a reference to Vauxhall Pleasure Gardens, rather than to Nine Elms terminal itself.

Early passengers using Nine Elms would likely have noted nearby Vauxhall Bridge, which at the time was an iron construction boasting nine arches (as opposed to today's bridge, which has five).

They may also have spotted the imposing Mill-bank Penitentiary, a notorious gaol that loomed on the opposite bank (on the site now occupied by Tate Britain), which for much of its life served as a holding centre for convicts awaiting a place on board a prison hulk bound for Australia.

Just opposite the station was Brunswick House, a mansion built in the 1750s; this would later be purchased by the railway and used as the headquarters for the huge goods yard and locomotive works that would eventually envelop Nine Elms. The building still stands today: dwarfed by modern architecture, it is the sole survivor from that earlier period.

Despite being isolated, Nine Elms was accessible to the rest of the city – then mainly concentrated on the northern banks of the Thames – thanks to an

Brunswick House, 2020.

omnibus service, a cab stand – located near the foot of Vauxhall Bridge – and, most notably, two piers that were situated just across the road from the terminal and offered steam-boat services to central London. These two jetties were named Railway Pier and Windmill Pier, the latter described by *Punch* magazine as being located beside 'the wreck of a windmill without any sails, and of which the whole of the top has either been stolen, blown away, burnt down, fallen into decay, or otherwise demolished'.

According to a report in *The Times* dated 10 July 1841, these jetties could be rather rowdy, due to the fact that they were operated by competing interests, a situation that encouraged touts to hustle for business. The report described these touts as being particularly coarse, stating that:

> *...their bawlings intermixed with the most ribald language, may be heard at a distance of a quarter of a mile... and it frequently happens when the trains come in, that the luggage of a passenger is roughly seized by one of these fellows and carried down to the rival pier, while the passenger, more especially if a female, is rudely dragged down the passage leading to the other.*

The Times also disclosed that the police apparently had no jurisdiction to prevent this behaviour, and blamed the authorities for allowing it to continue due to the supposed influence of a wealthy landowner who owned a 'large share in one of the piers in question.' For those passengers who did not intend to continue their journey to London – that was, of course, if they managed to evade being hauled away by the pier touts – the famous Vauxhall Pleasure Gardens were a short walk away.

Established in 1732, the gardens were particularly celebrated for their firework displays and hot-air balloon flights. Indeed, in the late summer of 1837, a balloon ascent was described in which the occupants were treated to a novel bird's-eye view of the London to Southampton line, then still under construction: 'We passed over Wandsworth, tracing with a precision that would have been delightful to an engineer, the course of the Southampton Railway nearly from Vauxhall to Kingston.'

As for the Nine Elms terminal building, this was a smart piece of architecture fashioned in the neo-classical style by Sir William Tite. Although demolished in the 1960s, its counterpart in Southampton, which is very similar in appearance, still stands, albeit in its current guise as a casino.

Southampton terminus.

Southampton terminus plaque.

In terms of how the Nine Elms terminus operated, the station was a relatively simple affair, as described in the following extract from a contemporary railway guide:

The entrance to the railway is by a plain but neat edifice, which leads to the offices, warehouses and other buildings occupying seven acres. The officers in attendance will point out the office for paying the fare and obtaining a check-ticket...From the booking-office the passenger is conducted to the trains, which are placed under a large roof supported by iron columns and well lighted at night.

In what could be considered a primitive forerunner to today's departure boards, a large bell was installed on the terminal's roof, which would clang for five minutes before a train was due to depart. A similar

Sir William Tite

The son of a Russian merchant, William Tite was born in London in 1798 and attended school in Hackney.

As well as designing the City of London's Royal Exchange and participating in the planning of large cemeteries such as Brookwood (which, as detailed in Chapter 4, would become closely linked with the history of Waterloo), Tite worked on numerous other railway projects including the design of many stations such as Chiswick, Kew Bridge, Yeovil, Exeter and Carlisle.

Sir William Tite.

system using handbells was employed on the line's smaller stations.

In typical Victorian fashion, the uniform worn by staff was exceptionally smart, and stringent rules existed to ensure it remained so. During the company's early years, the design was tweaked several times: in 1838 it consisted of a 'chocolate-coloured frock coat with very dark trousers'. This was soon swapped for a 'scarlet coat with silver buttons and lace collar', and then, six years later, the outfit had changed to 'one of blue, having a scarlet collar; blue trousers with two rows of scarlet piping.'

On 30 May 1838, just over a week after Nine Elms had opened, the facilities were pushed to their absolute limit. This was due to Derby Day, for which the L&SR had announced they would be laying on extra services to transport racegoers to Kingston, from where they could make the onward journey to Epsom Racecourse.

Unfortunately the company vastly underestimated the interest this would invoke, and around 5,000 Londoners descended upon Nine Elms. This unprecedented number resulted in a near riot as the booking counter was swamped, doors were torn from their hinges, and many eager travellers attempted to clamber through windows. As a result the police had to be called upon to restore order, and all services for that day were cancelled.

Other Stations to Woking

It is worth taking a moment to examine the other stations that opened on the L&SR's first section between London and Woking Common, as they played a key role in developing much of south-west London's commuter belt, an area that remains intrinsically linked to Waterloo today.

Wandsworth

Now long lost, Wandsworth station was situated on the northern tip of the Wandsworth Common cutting, approximately parallel to present-day Spencer Park, and just moments away from where the Clapham rail disaster occurred in December 1988. Wandsworth was renamed Clapham Common station, but closed in March 1863 following the opening of Clapham Junction.

Wimbledon

When it first opened in 1838, Wimbledon station consisted of a cluster of low buildings, and was based slightly south of its present site, on the opposite side of Wimbledon Bridge. The current station dates from the 1920s.

Kingston

Apparently the residents of 1830s Kingston were none too happy with the railway encroaching upon their land, meaning the station bearing their settlement's name was located more towards present-day Surbiton. Described as resembling a 'small cottage-like structure', this early station stood near King Charles Road. The area is now served by Surbiton station, an Art Deco masterpiece dating from 1937.

Ditton Marsh

Still in its original location, this station has gone by several names over the years. The original name, Ditton Marsh, was soon changed to Esher & Hampton Court, then Esher for Claremont, then Esher for Sandown Park. It has been known simply as Esher since 1913. The station was once home to a royal waiting room, and features two central platforms, which, along with the sealed-off street-level entrances, are now dilapidated.

Derelict stairwell, Esher.

Walton

Like Esher, Walton station – now known as Walton-on-Thames – remains at its original location and also has a disused island platform at its centre.

Weybridge

Weybridge, too, is at its original site, in the deep cutting that George Stephenson incorrectly predicted would bankrupt the L&SR.

Woking Common

Woking Common was a terminal for just a few months, the line being extended to Winchfield in September 1838. The station's name has since been shortened to Woking, and it is noted for its distinctive signal box, which was built in the 1930s and is now Grade II listed.

Renaming

As previously mentioned, the berthing facilities at Southampton had long been inferior to those offered by Portsmouth. The reason for this had been dictated by the geography of the Solent: it was simply easier for sailing ships to traverse the more open waters around Portsmouth.

Fortunately for the L&SR, the opening of their railway coincided with the rise of steamships (the SS *Great Western*, for example, made its maiden voyage between Bristol and New York in 1838, the same year in which L&SR opened), which were far better suited to Southampton. The subsequent increase in traffic naturally proved immensely beneficial for the fledgling line. Due to the L&SR's success, permission was quickly granted for a branch line linking Bishopstoke to Gosport as a means of serving Portsmouth.

Although the folk of Portsmouth were set to benefit from this, many residents were none too keen on having the name of their arch rival on the railway's branding. So as a compromise, it was agreed to switch the L&SR's name to the London & South Western Railway (L&SWR), a change that came into effect in June 1839.

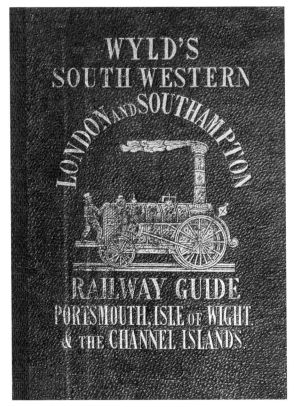

Wyld's Railway Guide, c.*1839.*

Pioneering Communication

As the early railways flourished, so too did another revolutionary invention: the electric telegraph. Both of these technologies were intertwined, with the first demonstration taking place on 25 July 1837 between the London & Birmingham Railway's Euston to Camden Town section. Over the next few years telegraph lines were installed alongside relatively short stretches of track on the GWR and the London & Blackwall Railway. However, it was on the L&SWR that the first truly long-distance network made its debut.

The primary function of the L&SWR's wire was to serve the military – as an efficient way of exchanging messages between London and the naval headquarters at Portsmouth – and was installed by William Fothergill Cooke and Charles Wheatstone, the two men who had pioneered the technology on the London to Birmingham line. Their system was chosen over another design trialled by Scottish inventor Alexander Bain in 1844 between Nine Elms and Wimbledon. Although Bain lost out, his invention was still extremely impressive in that it utilized an electric printer, very much like an early fax machine.

Early Incidents

With the technology still something of a novelty, and an almost complete disregard for what we today would term 'health and safety', railways in the early nineteenth century posed significant dangers, and the line that would eventually find its way to Waterloo had its fair share of mishaps.

Unsurprisingly, the earliest incidents along the route between London and Southampton occurred during its construction. In November 1836, for example, a gang of navvies was buried alive whilst loading wagons at an excavation site near Woking. Thanks to their strength, three of the men managed to claw their way out of the rubble and haul their colleagues to safety, although this wasn't enough to save a Mr John Tingles, whose head 'was literally crushed to pieces'.

When passenger services began operating in 1838, guards would keep an eye on the track and blow a whistle when the train approached a curve or populated area, or indeed if they spotted trespassers on the track. Despite this measure, accidents were commonplace.

One of the first fatal incidents to occur during public service took place on 8 June 1838, just a few weeks after the line had opened. It was reported that two friends were wandering about on the tracks between Walton and Woking, and although warned of the danger, took no heed. They were still on the rails when a 'double train of carriages and wagons came up, and before they could get clear out of the way the engine wheel caught them, by which means they were prostrated and the vehicles passed over them.'

As a result, one of the men perished after being 'dreadfully mangled', although somehow his friend managed to survive.

That same day, two employees of the L&SR, described as having 'drunk too freely', had positioned themselves between the two sets of rails, having apparently forgotten they'd attached a rope between an engine and a set of wagons which stood opposite '...in consequence of which they were knocked down by the rope, and thrown under the whole of the wagons. They were dreadfully injured, and but little hope remains of their recovery.'

Even more bizarrely, in July 1842, one unfortunate fellow named John Mitchell happened to doze off on the tracks at Woking Common after a heavy drinking session. He was subsequently struck by a train, which resulted in his leg being 'torn off and thrown some distance'. Mitchell was pulled on board the train with a view to seeking medical help, but died before reaching Nine Elms.

As well as these hapless folk struck on the rails, there were a number of incidents of a mechanical nature, too. On the 17 May 1840, for example, one train was derailed after striking debris on the line. Although there were no fatalities, a number of passengers suffered concussion, two carriages were 'shattered to pieces', and one of the engine operators nearly had his leg 'severed from his body'.

More seriously, on the foggy evening of 17 October 1840, a fatal collision occurred at the Nine Elms terminal when a train ploughed into the back of another. This resulted in the death of Catherine Andrews, who was returning home with a friend after a day trip to Hampton Court. One reporter, upon examining the damaged carriages, remarked that their design seemed to 'offer very little security against concussions of even a comparatively slight nature', whilst another correspondent made the angry claim that the railway's managers seemed to harbour a 'frightful indifference to human life'.

On a lighter note, a derailment occurred in March 1841 when the *Tartar* – the engine that had been commanded by Joseph Locke on one of the railway's private demonstration days – came off the rails, resulting in its wheels being 'deeply imbedded in the earth'. This was most inconvenient, as the engine was due to haul the evening mail train, so it was fortunate that the crew managed to heave it back and have the engine running again in just twenty minutes – a situation that would be unprecedented today.

Overcrowding

Despite early reports praising the L&SR for its comfortable carriages, overcrowding appears to have been a significant – and dangerous – problem, which quickly materialized thanks to the railway's popularity. Writing to *The Times* on 9 July 1839, one gentleman described his attempts to board a train at Kingston during the morning rush hour:

On the arrival of the half-past 8 o'clock train this morning at the Kingston station…where upwards of 50 passengers were waiting to be conveyed to town, it was found that there was not room for one of them, the number of carriages, which ought to have been increased on a Monday morning, having been reduced below the usual average. As Kingston is considered the very best station on the railway, this, to say the least of it, was gross inattention, as

it disappointed many who have to be at public offices by a certain hour…

On a spare truck 21 passengers were wedged, and 13 were clustered outside a stage coach. Several were obliged to sit round, and on this truck I observed one respectable female underneath the body of the coach. None of the passengers will really forget the sensation occasioned by the passengers on the top of the stage coach stooping when passing under the lower bridges – the most trifling jerk, or the slightest giddiness or nervousness, would have occasioned a fearful accident.

Onward Progress

After just a few years, the L&SWR's popularity meant that the terminal at Nine Elms had become a victim of its own success: the end of the line being in what was then a remote London suburb, coupled with the fact that passengers had to make their onward journey by ferry, cab or omnibus, was beginning to prove most inconvenient.

It was time to take the tracks closer to town.

CHAPTER 2

Onwards to Waterloo

From the outset the L&SWR had never envisioned Nine Elms as a permanent terminal, and by the early 1840s it was already apparent that their burgeoning success was indeed fast making the site redundant.

As well as passengers and freight from the increasingly popular Southampton Docks pouring into the terminal, the stations on the line closer to London – in particular Ditton Marsh, Kingston, Wimbledon and Wandsworth – had created a bustling commuter belt, of which Nine Elms was the head. Whilst good for ticket sales, the overcrowding that ensued did little for efficient running or customer satisfaction.

Nine Elms was marooned in what many then considered to be an isolated area, and those wishing to continue their journey towards central London had limited options. There were the two river steamers (named *Citizen* and *Bridegroom*), but the sheer number of passengers often necessitated a lengthy wait, often upwards of thirty minutes. Taking the omnibus was a second option, although this was slow and uncomfortable. Thirdly, passengers could hail a cab, but this was expensive and involved negotiating pricey toll gates.

Traffic along the L&SWR was also about to increase with the addition of extra commuter routes, which themselves played a major role in forging the Waterloo we know today. This process commenced with the Richmond Railway.

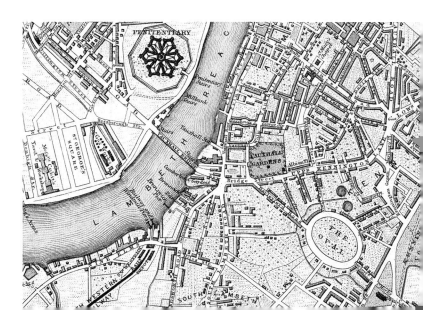

Nine Elms and the surrounding area in the 1840s; the L&SWR terminal can be seen in the bottom left-hand corner.

First Attempt

In 1836 – shortly before railway mania truly took hold, and just two years after permission to build the L&SWR had been granted – a prospectus for a railway linking Richmond to London was published. This was dubbed the 'City of London & Richmond Railway' (CL&RR), and sought permission to create a line from Richmond that would terminate close to the southern end of Southwark Bridge. It was also hoped a branch line would be added, leaving the main route at Battersea, from where it would cross the Thames and head up through west London, terminating at Harlesden Green.

There was considerable opposition to this project, both in Richmond and Southwark. As one report noted:

...the route will have to proceed through a great number of crowded streets; and hundreds of houses, manufactories, &c, will have to be destroyed, causing a vast deal of inconvenience and loss. The length of the viaduct necessary for this railway will be six miles.

This was in stark contrast to the L&SWR, which had chosen a relatively pastoral route with the Nine Elms terminus sited on vacant land.

In January 1837 Richmond residents held a meeting to oppose the CL&RR, their main bones of contention being that the railway would involve a 'needless and uncalled for invasion of private property', that it would be a nuisance, and that Richmond already enjoyed 'rapid and easy communication' with London via road and river connections. There was also vocal opposition from the residents of Blackfriars, who did not wish to see the tracks encroach upon their neighbourhood. Consequently, a group was formed to petition parliament.

To counteract these protests, those behind the CL&RR quietly – and audaciously – renamed their bill the 'Southwark & Hammersmith Railway' as a means of throwing petitioners off the scent. The ruse worked, and those wishing to oppose the bill in parliament missed the debate – easily done when so many similarly named bills were doing the rounds.

However, this deception was quickly discovered, and in April 1837 parliament decided that, although not fraudulent, this sly move was in contravention to the rules of the House. In the same session it was declared that the chances of the CL&RR being granted permission would have been an 'utter impossibility' anyway, and the bill died a quiet death.

Reviving the Richmond Railway

In 1844 a group of businessmen decided to revisit the idea of connecting Richmond and London by rail. This time, perhaps in mind of the bullish and somewhat scandalous behaviour that had occurred seven years previously, the plans were made far more palatable. The new prospectus was labelled the 'Richmond & West End Junction Railway' (R&WEJR), and proposed the construction of a line through Mortlake, Barnes and Putney – that is, just north of, and roughly parallel to, the route followed by the London to Southampton line.

Rather than plough through densely populated Southwark, it was now suggested that once the line reached Wandsworth at an area known as Falconbridge – now Clapham Junction – it would link up with the L&SWR and share the tracks to Nine Elms. It was also hoped the line would eventually cross the Thames and establish a terminal at a site close to Hungerford Bridge.

Interestingly, the project's supporters argued that such a railway was bound to flourish because at the time, ninety-eight omnibuses ran between Richmond and London per day, thus proving the route's popularity. In 1836, those opposing the original proposal had used similar figures to argue *against* the idea, insisting that Richmond was already well connected. No doubt, however, the directors of the R&WEJR assumed (correctly) that many coach and river passengers would be tempted to switch to a faster, smoother link if one were provided.

From the outset the L&SWR were supportive of the idea, and agreed to cooperate. There was one condition, however: the L&SWR insisted they would take charge of any extension across the Thames from Nine

Clapham Junction was originally called Falconbridge, named after a local pub, the current incarnation of which dates from the 1880s.

Elms. This was readily agreed, and on 21 July 1845 parliament gave the go-ahead for the new section of railway to be built between Richmond and Clapham, declaring it was now 'lawful to enter upon, take and use such lands as necessary'.

L&SWR engineering stalwart Joseph Locke was once again employed to oversee the project. As it transpired, the task was relatively simple – 'comparatively trifling', as one report put it. Only 6 miles (9.7km) of line had to be built, and with the terrain being smooth and flat, there were few headaches for Locke. The main engineering feat was the construction of a

viaduct at Wandsworth, built to carry the line over the River Wandle.

Between Richmond and the junction with the L&SWR, stations were built at Mortlake, Barnes, Putney and Wandsworth Town. Each of these station buildings was fashioned in a smart Tudor style by architect John Thomas Emmett. Sadly, only Barnes maintains its original building today.

Construction of the R&WEJR was swift, and on 23 July 1846 it was formally opened when a sixteen-car train pulled out of Nine Elms and 'moved slowly along the main line of the South Western for two miles; it then turned off to the right and proceeded at a more rapid rate along the newly constructed portion to Richmond.'

Upon arrival at Richmond, passengers on this inaugural service were met with 'a gay appearance decked out in flags with "Welcome" in large characters... while the ringing of bells and the strains of music ushered in the first train.' The day concluded with a large banquet at The Castle, which was attended by 400 guests.

The following year, the R&WEJR was fully absorbed by the L&SWR, and after experience showed that it was problematic for services to share the line, extra rails were laid down, meaning that four sets of tracks now entered Nine Elms. This addition would also facilitate the now-inevitable extension from the terminal.

Barnes station.

The Guildford Junction Railway

In 1838 it was suggested that a branch from the L&SWR's station at Woking could provide a link with Guildford. This proposal, published under the title *The Guildford Junction Railway* (GJR), was given the go-ahead by parliament in April 1844.

The GJR's backers initially wanted their line to be constructed using a system developed by William Prosser. To modern sensibilities especially, Prosser's design was most unusual in that the rails and wheels were made of wood, the idea being that it was cheaper. On Prosser's system, which was demonstrated at an experimental track on Wimbledon Common in 1845, the locomotive had three wheel sizes: the large and medium were smooth like cartwheels, whilst the smaller wheels were flanged and angled at 45 degrees in order to grip the track.

For passengers wishing to travel beyond Woking, this would have required switching trains, as Prosser's system was entirely incompatible with the L&SWR's more conventional network. Because of this, the L&SWR declared they would only support the GJR if Prosser's system were ditched. This was agreed to, and it was also decided to sell the GJR to the L&SWR for £75,000.

The line was quickly built and ready for business on 5 May 1845, thus connecting Nine Elms to Guildford. The initially short branch from Woking to Guildford was the first section on what would later become the main line to Portsmouth.

Prosser's wooden system meanwhile briefly saw use on New Zealand's Southland Railway.

Planning for Waterloo

Whilst these expansions were underway, the L&SWR were also gearing up to extend from Nine Elms to a site beside either Waterloo Bridge or Hungerford Market (the latter now being the approximate location of the later built Charing Cross station).

Planning had begun in the autumn of 1844 when Joseph Locke and William Tite carried out a survey of the surrounding area. In doing so, they pinpointed a site south of the Thames, which bordered York Road and was described as being 'the only spot in that district not covered with houses, as well adapted for a terminus'. They also plotted the route of the expected line from Nine Elms to the proposed site.

For several days in June 1845, the case for extending the line was put before a parliamentary committee. Here it was explained that, if permitted, the extension would be constructed on a long brick viaduct – 'at an immense cost' to the L&SWR – in a similar vein to the L&GR. Although there was some admittance that the project was opposed in certain quarters, the L&SWR stated their belief that the extension would be of such benefit to the public that 'the thought of all other considerations would be lost in the comparison of the conflicting interests'.

The first witness questioned by the committee was a Mr Reede, former secretary to the L&SWR. Rather haughtily, Reede stated that the 'advantages of the proposed extension were too numerous to detail, and too obvious to require explanation'. Nevertheless he proceeded to furnish details:

> In the first place, a man on leaving the station at Nine Elms, in his carriage, had to cross Vauxhall-bridge, for which he would be mulcted of 8d. toll, and before he had put the change in his pocket would have to hand over another shilling in payment of a turnpike toll of 11d.

Further to this, Reede added that, in his opinion, the property through which the line would go was 'of the most worthless character' and that he 'did not believe that a more miserable locality was to be found in the metropolis'.

This view was supported by Mr Mangles MP, who complained that it had cost him as much to get from Nine Elms to Hyde Park in a cab as it did to convey him the whole distance from Guildford to London by the South Western Railway. Naturally, Mr Mangles backed the L&SWR's proposals.

VICTORIAN STYLE

In 1845, as the addition of branch lines to Richmond and Guildford bolstered the L&SWR's popularity further, the company saw fit to construct a new fleet of carriages. In November that year, *The Times* provided a detailed insight as to what they looked like:

> *In the first-class carriage…safety, convenience and beauty appear to have been severely studied in drawing out the design. The seats are formed with springs, and the back linings are provided with the same, they being so elastic as to afford the greatest possible comfort, and, in the event of any accident, will no doubt cause a great reduction in the shock that might be consequent.*
>
> *In addition to the usual door and side glasses, there is a light frame composed of very fine wire gauze which is very neatly painted, and which, when it is found necessary to lower the glass for the admission of air, may be raised up, and so answer the twofold purpose of partially admitting air and of avoiding dust.*
>
> *The interior is also provided with two lamps of neat workmanship and is lined with blue cloth, furnished with broad lace of handsome pattern. The body is painted and varnished in the usual style, the two doors bearing the company's arms. The carriage is mounted upon painted wooden wheels, which appear to be of a superior construction…*
>
> *Turning to the second-class carriage…side-lights and doors have been provided similar to those of the first class; but it has not the gauze frame. The third-class carriage is of a very serviceable make, no doubt, but still maintains a degree of plebeian character.*

Several years later, in 1848, another set of fresh carriages, designed to specifically coincide with the opening of the Nine Elms extension, were revealed to be 'of a peculiarly noiseless and easily moving structure – artistically decorated too, with panels of the scenery'.

Opposition

As noted at the committee, there were folk who were against an extension being built through Lambeth. Some months prior to the committee, on 6 January 1845, a public meeting (which the *London Evening Standard* described as being a 'very stormy one') was held at the Horns Tavern, Kennington, where local landowners gathered to voice their concerns. The case against the extension was eloquently presented by a barrister named Mr Chandless:

> *The simple question before them was, whether a railway which already had a terminus at Nine Elms, which was already within a reasonable distance of the heart of the city, should be allowed, at the cost of great private injury, to have another terminus at Hungerford Bridge; so that it was, in fact, a mere question of a saving of time, to the amount of 10 minutes or a quarter of an hour, and a little expense to those persons who travelled by the South-Western Railway.*
>
> *And for so paltry a purpose it was proposed to destroy much private property, to injure more in such a manner as to render it nearly worthless, and to drive hundreds of families to seek new homes, and others new places of business, probably in a neighbourhood where they were unknown.*
>
> *The proposed line was to be carried along arches all the way; it would, in fact, be like building a wall along the whole line, shutting*

out light and air from all those residing in the neighbourhood, and interrupting the means of communication between all places on either side of it. Wherever this had been already done, the depreciation of the property in the immediate neighbourhood had been very great.

To illustrate this last point, the railway arches along the Minories (built close to the Tower of London by the London & Blackwell Railway in 1840) and Bermondsey Street (by the L&GR in 1836) were indicated as examples of what some considered to be an urban blight.

At the same meeting, a 'well-dressed and good-humoured working man' called John Roberts stepped up to voice his support for the scheme. John was of the opinion that, as the line was pencilled in to run through a 'filthy, stinking, and unwholesome district', it would do much good and provide employment for many thousands – including himself. His words were met with laughter, with some in the crowd calling out 'you are paid for coming here'!

Trafalgar Station?

Although the L&SWR were primarily aiming for the York Road site in the mid-1840s, there were hopes that the extension would eventually cross the Thames and settle at a terminal close to Hungerford Market. With this potential site located just moments away from what was then a very newly laid out Trafalgar Square, it is probable that, had the L&SWR's plan succeeded, London would have gained a terminal named after the Napoleonic Wars' most celebrated naval battle.

However, any thought of using the site was blocked by Hugh Percy, the 3rd Duke of Northumberland. This was due to the fact that his grand property, Northumberland House, stood on the proposed spot (on the south-eastern tip of Trafalgar Square) and he refused to budge.

Northumberland House, which was particularly noted for its lavish marble staircase, dated back to 1605, a time when it was fashionable for those of nobility to build themselves a riverside residence in order to be near the monarch. Today, Somerset House is the only surviving example of this trend, although other grand properties live on in names such as Essex Street, Surrey Street and, of course, Northumberland Avenue.

There were some reports in the press of the L&SWR's attempts to obtain this lucrative plot. In October 1845, *The London Illustrated News* noted that 'a treaty for the purchase of Northumberland

Looking towards the site of the former Northumberland House.

House is going on between its ducal proprietor and the South-Western.' In reference to this story, the *American Railroad Journal* added, 'the excellence of this site for a west end terminus is superlative'. This opinion was shared by one contributor to the *Westminster Review*, who claimed that once Hugh Percy had been evicted, 'the finest of all sites for a railway station' would be acquired.

Punch magazine, on the other hand, knowing that any attempt to win over the Duke was futile, quipped that the L&SWR should purchase the National Gallery instead as it was 'totally unfit for its present purpose and to sell it to a railway company is the best thing that could be done'.

Northumberland House was finally swept away in the 1860s, by which point Hugh Percy had long since passed away – he died in 1847, one year before Waterloo station opened – as had his successor, Algernon Percy. The title was now held by the 5th Duke, George Percy, who, following a serious fire at Northumberland House, agreed to sell the damaged property to the Metropolitan Board of Works for the then immense sum of £500,000.

Construction Begins

In the grand scheme of things, opposition to the L&SWR's extension proved inconsequential, and on 31 July 1845 parliament passed the Metropolitan Extension Act permitting construction of the necessary viaduct from Nine Elms to York Road – the site where Waterloo station stands today – to commence. The building work was contracted to Messrs Lee & Co.

Although the L&SWR were unsuccessful in their attempts to secure a site north of the Thames, they had little trouble in purchasing the plot of land that lay adjacent to York Road and close to the foot of Waterloo Bridge (as recommended by Locke and Tite in 1844). This was acquired in 1846, and, using what was initially 10 acres (16ha), they announced their plan to erect a 'commodious station' on the site.

At the time this area was sparsely populated. An examination of maps from the early nineteenth century reveals a smattering of small buildings and businesses, through the middle of which ran a lane called Vine Street. The plot's southern border – marked by Westminster Bridge Road – was home to the Lying-in Hospital, one of Britain's first maternity units founded by Dr John Leake (who would later have a road named after him: this now runs beneath Waterloo station).

Several taverns stood in the area, as did a wine and vinegar maker named Beaufoy and two calico printers. Most intriguing of all was the presence of Dr James's Laboratory, which would have been located approximately between where platforms 10 to 19 now stand. Dr Robert James was a quack who in the 1740s developed a powder that he claimed could cure everything from scurvy to gout. This dubious cure was surprisingly popular and sold long after his death.

By November 1847 it was reported that the area – summed up at the time as being 'vacant ground, to a great extent occupied as hay-stalls and cow-yards and by dung heaps, and similar nuisances' – had been cleared, and that building work was due to commence.

Although plans for the station were grand, it was not initially envisioned as a terminal. Instead it was considered more of a stepping stone on a route eventually leading to London's Square Mile. Indeed, on 27 June 1846, permission was granted for the L&SWR to construct a potential extension from Waterloo to London Bridge. But the following month the Metropolitan Railway Commission – alarmed at the rapid expansion of the railways, and fearing that

Map of the Waterloo area before the arrival of the railway. The plot earmarked for the terminus is outlined in red.

countless tracks and viaducts were about to swamp the capital's crowded environs – advised that no lines should be permitted to encroach upon central London.

Nevertheless, as we shall see, the L&SWR's desire to reach the city's financial heart remained resolute throughout the nineteenth century.

Construction south of the river was given much freer rein, and as the months passed, the extension from Nine Elms to Waterloo – which involved the construction of some 300 arches and a number of iron bridges – proceeded swiftly. The most famous example of this speediness was encapsulated by the skew arch over Miles Street, a description of which was given in *The London Illustrated News* in March 1847:

> *Most of the arches on the western portion of it are already formed; many of them have to cross wide streets: the one crossing Miles-street, South Lambeth, has sprung into existence as if by magic.*
>
> *It is a skew arch, of very difficult build being on one side 48 feet whilst on the other, it is only 38 feet wide, and forming a curve of 54 feet span; it required for its completion 90,000 bricks; and, notwithstanding its peculiarities, this immense arch of brickwork was begun, pointed, dressed and finished in the almost incredible short time of forty-five hours! What would the builders in Sir Christopher Wren's day have said had such a feat been required of them?*

Once complete, each of the viaduct's arches was covered with Seysell asphalt to make them neat and waterproof, for it was correctly predicted that these spaces would attract business use.

There was also some brief discussion as to whether or not the arches could be utilized for residential purposes – this had been trialled some years before on the L&GR – though it was concluded, with some humour, that this would be impractical as the smoke from the tenants' coal fires would cause discomfort to passengers travelling above.

Miles Street arch.

Crime on the L&SWR

With its visible wealth, the L&SWR inevitably became a target for criminals. One particularly lucrative ruse – described by one newspaper as an 'ingeniously concocted and ably carried out system of plunder' – was to pillage moving goods trains. One gang in particular, led by two men named Joseph Raymond and Charles Fidler, specialized in this hustle.

According to witnesses, these crooks – who targeted late-night services under cover of darkness – would have one man stationed on the train. As it rumbled along, this character would pick out all manner of goods, including 'chests of tea, bales of silk, trusses of drapery goods, rolls of carpet... umbrellas and parasols, carcasses of pigs... butter... hams and large quantities of broad cloth'; these would be tossed off the train and scooped up minutes later by track-side accomplices. When the gang were caught red-handed, they were in the process of collecting the loot near Stewarts Lane, Battersea.

During the course of their spree, Raymond and Fidler's gang stole an estimated £1,000 worth of items – over £100,000 in today's money. At the trial in July 1847, it was said that if all those who had received these stolen goods were to be brought forwards, 'half of London would have to attend'.

Tinworth Street arches.

Many years later, one of the arches on the Nine Elms to Waterloo viaduct – a unit off Tinworth Street – was involved in a far more grievous crime: the Braybrook Street massacre. This appalling incident occurred on a residential street in Acton in August 1966 when Harry Roberts, John Duddy and John Witney were approached by police whilst sitting in their clapped-out Vanguard van. The officers were just carrying out a simple tax-disc check, but Roberts panicked and opened fire. In the ensuing chaos, three policemen were killed in cold blood.

Following the triple murder, the gang sped to Vauxhall where the vehicle was quickly stashed in a garage located in the Tinworth Street arch. So desperate was the driver to conceal the vehicle that he scraped the wall as the van lurched in. The noise attracted the attention of a witness, who was able to alert police to the vehicle's location, thus securing vital clues and evidence.

As building work progressed, some Lambeth residents continued to voice their opposition. This came to a head in January 1848, when a meeting was called after 'finding that a very serious nuisance was about to be perpetrated'. The issue in question was the bridge over Church Road (now Lambeth Road), which, rather than having a single-span arch like others on the line, was about to be given a large brick pier centred in the middle of the road.

There was particular concern over this as the structure was just moments away from Lambeth Palace, and it was feared it would spoil the appearance of the approach (in fact this aspect remains to this day, and it does look somewhat unwieldy!)

Those opposed to the pier's construction believed that the work had been sanctioned due to ignorance, and hoped to bring action by citing the pier as a nuisance and an obstruction of the Queen's Highway. In their defence, the L&SWR – represented by a Mr Tate – declared that the company were 'most anxious to meet the parish in an amicable spirit'.

Mr Tate went on to explain how the company had, within the parish, provided a new school house, opened up new roads, and improved the area overall, and that it would be unfair to drag the L&SWR into expensive litigation at a point when the works were so far advanced. Added to this, a surveyor named Mr Hodson warned residents that it was futile to embark upon 'useless and expensive litigation'. Upon hearing these arguments, the opposition folded.

In contrast to this attitude, another meeting of local residents was held in April 1848, in which it was conceded that the 'railway company had acted very liberally towards the parish', and that 'every concession had been followed by corresponding advantages to the parish'.

Lambeth Road pier.

Final Preparations

By June 1848 the extension from Nine Elms to Waterloo was complete, with the final cost coming in at £2 million. This was an astronomical sum for the time, and demonstrated the faith that the Victorians now put in the railways. Built rapidly, like the rest of the line, the new terminal – the first Waterloo station – was originally named Waterloo Bridge station; the title was not officially shortened until 1886. However, even before then, many referred to the station simply as 'Waterloo', and for simplicity, that is how I shall refer to it from this point onwards.

In February 1848 the L&SWR held a board meeting at Nine Elms: it had to be conducted in one of the company's spacious warehouses due to the huge turnout. Here it was announced that:

> *The arching for the station was rapidly advancing, and a sufficient area would be raised to the proper level by the end of the present month, so as to enable the architect to commence the permanent booking and other offices.*

By June, as predicted at this meeting, the new station, perched on a number of arches to combat marshy terrain, was indeed ready.

Before the extension could open to the public, an inspection by the Board of Trade was required. The first of these occurred on Wednesday 29 June 1848, when a government inspector, accompanied by engineer Joseph Locke, examined the line.

During the course of the day, two locomotives made their way along the tracks from Vauxhall to Waterloo, with particular importance being placed on examining the iron bridges. As tests were being conducted on the bridge spanning Westminster Bridge Road – the longest on the extension – a 'good deal of interest' was excited amongst locals.

It was hoped the line would open on the following Saturday. However, there were slight concerns over certain aspects, and after some alterations were made, a second test was conducted on Thursday 6 July. This was overseen by Captain Simmonds of the Royal Engineers, who was accompanied by the

Waterloo Bridge

The first Waterloo Bridge, after which the L&SWR terminal was originally named, was designed by John Rennie; it was the fourth to cross the Thames, the first three being London, Westminster and Blackfriars. It was originally going to be called the Strand Bridge, and construction commenced in 1811. Four years later, whilst the bridge was still being built, the Battle of Waterloo was fought and won, leading the Strand Bridge Company to rename their structure in honour of the victory.

Waterloo Bridge finally opened on 18 June 1817. It boasted nine columns and was considered a marvel; the Italian sculptor, Antonio Canova, described it as 'the noblest bridge in the world... alone worth coming to London to see'.

Waterloo Bridge, 1846.

Rennie's bridge survived until the 1930s, when structural problems necessitated its replacement. Stones from Rennie's old structure were sent to various parts of the world including New Zealand, where the remains were used to forge a memorial to 'Paddy the Wanderer', a faithful little dog who spent his life roaming the wharves around Wellington Harbour during the Great Depression.

The second bridge was designed by Sir Giles Gilbert Scott, and due to the fact that it was constructed during World War II, a large labour force of women was used.

Today, Waterloo Bridge is generally considered to offer one of the finest views of London. It can be spotted in numerous films, including the end scenes of both *Alfie* (1967) and, rather appropriately, *Train-spotting* (1996).

railway's chairman, W. Chapman, and several other officers. During this inspection, Captain Simmonds examined each of the iron bridges thoroughly, as well as the 'arched terrace of the station'.

When it came to Westminster Bridge Road, however, the level of road traffic was deemed too busy – the process required the positioning of several sturdy rods beneath the bridge in order to gauge any potential shift in its structure. Because of this, it was decided to return the following day, bright and early at 6am. That morning a no doubt bleary-eyed Mr Kerr – the resident engineer – and Mr Gooch – the superintendent of locomotive traffic – met Captain Simmonds and proceeded with the Westminster Bridge Road trial, which was described thus:

Four of the largest engines and tenders were placed on the crown of the bridge at once, and afterwards moved backwards and forwards simultaneously. This test is considered a most severe one, but the noble edifice bore it gallantly.

Following this stringent experiment, the structure met with the Captain's approval, and the opening of the extension was set for Tuesday 11 July 1848.

Waterloo Bridge Station Opens

In the short span between the final trial and Waterloo's opening, last-minute work was carried out in 'prepping' the station, adjusting rails and 'bringing the furniture and fittings from Nine Elms'.

The very first train to arrive on the historic morning of 11 July 1848 was a seven-carriage mail service, hauled by an engine named *Hornet*, which had departed Southampton shortly after 1am carrying forty passengers. It entered Waterloo at 4.30am where, despite the unbearably early hour, hundreds of workmen and officials were busy finalizing last-minute alterations and so were present to witness the event – it was reported they received the train with a loud cheer.

As the day progressed, services continued to flow in and out of the station without incident – although passengers had to be careful not to trip over tools or building materials whilst workers hastily cleared up. Five days after Waterloo opened, the *London Weekly Chronicle* provided readers with a detailed account:

The temporary station, though constructed entirely of wood, is really a handsome and commodious building. The great booking office is 70 feet long by 30 feet wide. There are ladies' waiting-rooms on a superb scale, and the usual accommodation for clerks, superintendents, parcels, lamps and all the countless etceteras of a station on a most extensive scale…

For the convenience of our readers we beg to explain that the access for passengers going from London is by the inclined road, and entrance in the Waterloo bridge road, the southernmost of the two entrances nearest the Victoria Theatre.

For foot passengers at present the access is the same; but in a day or two there will be an additional access by a footpath from York Road, at the end of Vine Street. For passengers arriving there are several exits which it is not necessary to specify, as they are all apparent, or readily pointed out by the servants of the company.

To aid access to and from the station further, the L&SWR provided space for 100 cabs. Another account, published less than two weeks after the station's opening, enthusiastically described the positive impact Waterloo was having on the local area:

Since the opening of the station…an air of bustle has pervaded the whole street [Waterloo Road]; numberless cabs and carriages, from early dawn to midnight, are pouring in from all directions; whilst the omnibuses which the district hither hardly maintained, are keeping a rich harvest from the influx of railway travellers.

The shopkeepers have left off wearing their hands in their pockets, and bustle about as though they had something to do. It is like the infusion of new blood into a patient expiring from atrophy; new life and renewed vigour are at once apparent in every fibre, and activity and hope take the places of stupor and indifference. The railway has produced this restored animation, and the railway and nothing else is talked of from one end of 'the road' to the other.

Waterloo Bridge station had arrived. And it was about to get even bigger.

Snake, *built at Nine Elms in 1843; this locomotive was one of the first to serve the L&SWR's new terminal at Waterloo.*

CHAPTER 3

Chaos Comes to York Road

When it opened in the summer of 1848, Waterloo station was a far smaller affair compared to the landmark we know today. In all it spanned an area of approximately half an acre, with its footprint covering the space now occupied by modern-day platforms 7 to 12.

AN EARLY VIEW

Although photography was in use in the capital by the 1840s, no photographs of the original Waterloo station as it looked upon opening appear to have survived, if indeed any were taken at all. Instead we have to go by detailed engravings from the time: these depict a modest building with a neat, simple roof constructed from iron, like the columns supporting it. Tucked to the side was a point of pedestrian access: a tall, wooden, shed-like structure, around which wound a covered staircase.

Opposite this stairwell was a long, sloped ramp providing access for horse-drawn vehicles. It is only

Waterloo station, 1848.

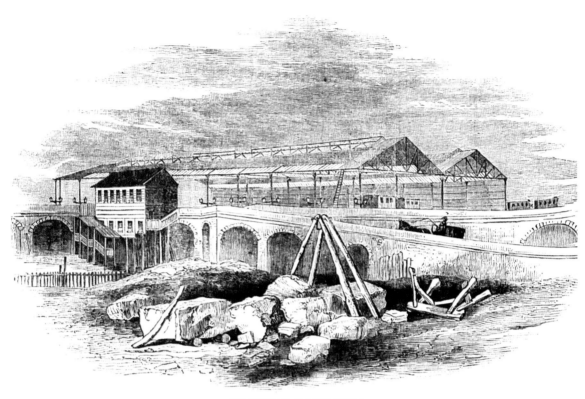

THE WATERLOO RAILWAY-STATION.

Alternative view of Waterloo, 1848, from Lady's Own Newspaper.

the long line of sturdy arches supporting the tracks and platforms that hint at the mighty terminal that would later evolve on this spot. Although not seen in these sketches, another feature of early Waterloo was the 'Crow's Nest', a wooden signal box that perched over the platforms.

The Running Lines

In the early days, trains entering the station did so under a system that sounds decidedly archaic by today's standards. As a train approached Waterloo, it would come to a halt at a narrow, timber platform just outside the station, close to Westminster Bridge Road. This platform was not for alighting: it was occupied by a guard who would collect passengers' tickets. As he did so, a rope would be hooked to the engine.

Once cleared, the train would slowly move forwards on this 'running line': upon reaching around 10mph (16km/h), the rope would be pulled, disconnecting the engine and thus allowing it to be marshalled towards a siding. The carriages meanwhile were rolled towards one of the station's four platforms under the control of the guard's brake. The platform number to which the carriages were assigned was signalled by a corresponding sequence of strikes on a gong, triggered by a lever as the train entered.

This process, which remained in use well into the 1860s, sometimes proved to be a bumpy experience. One evening in October 1850, for example, a mishap caused the buffer van to ram heavily into a carriage containing twenty-five passengers. Although the collision wasn't serious, it did cause the occupants to be 'suddenly thrown from their seats in all directions', and a number of minor injuries were sustained.

What Became of Nine Elms

Although the L&SWR shifted their terminus further north, Nine Elms remained an important depot for decades, the site for huge locomotive, carriage and wagon workshops along with a sprawling goods depot. For some years Nine Elms also accommodated Queen Victoria's private station, which faced Wandsworth Road, opposite Wyvil Road.

Most curiously, in 1850 a bizarre train named *The Impulsoria* was trialled at Nine Elms. Invented by Clemente Masserano, this train was horse-driven, with the animals walking on a treadmill. The design never caught on.

The Impulsoria.

It's Only Temporary

It must be remembered that in the late 1840s Waterloo was considered a stop-gap, and it was anticipated that the line would soon be extended towards either Hungerford Bridge or London Bridge. Indeed, the L&SWR had purchased property in the vicinity of London Bridge to the tune of £12,000 to facilitate an extension.

It wasn't just the L&SWR who desired further growth. In 1850, for instance, an independent pamphlet was published, which described an extension from Waterloo to London Bridge as being vital in 'promoting European trade'.

Because of the prevailing belief that Waterloo would soon become just another regular station on the line, its early buildings – such as the ticket and telegraph offices – were temporary wooden structures. These makeshift facilities were located alongside the now vanished Vine Street, which curved around the station's north-western end. The L&SWR also moved their headquarters to a temporary office at Waterloo, although for a time, some meetings continued to be held at Nine Elms.

If a prospective traveller wished to purchase tickets in advance, particularly for a special excursion service, advertisements in the press from the period – often presented by the station's very Dickensian-sounding general manager, Cornelius Stovin – stated that it was possible to buy the said tickets at a number of locations around the city. These included the 'Universal Office' at Regent Circus, along with a number of taverns: the 'Swan with Two Necks' (Lad Lane, now Gresham Street), the 'Spread Eagle' (Gracechurch Street), the 'Blue Boar' (Holborn) and the 'Golden Cross' (Charing Cross).

NEW STATION UNDER PRESSURE

Similar to the original Nine Elms terminus, Waterloo promptly found itself at the head of an ever-increasing network, with lines both close to London (such as Chertsey and Hampton Court) and further afield quickly opening up. A further boost in traffic occurred after the L&SWR carried out work to improve Southampton Docks.

Certain events also put the new station under pressure. Shortly after Nine Elms had opened in 1838, one of the first challenges to present itself was the issue of handling huge crowds heading to Derby Day at Epsom Racecourse. The situation at Waterloo was no different: in May 1851 a report in *The Morning Chronicle* describing racegoers who had opted to travel via Waterloo rather than London Bridge, ran as follows:

> *From an early hour in the morning, the door of the station was besieged by thousands of persons, and as the day wore on, no-one who saw the Waterloo-station and the eager throng who were pushing, and struggling, and shouting for places, would have supposed that there was any other mode of approaching Epsom than by the round-about course to Kingston.*
>
> *And the confusion that existed at the ticket-office was not very likely to subside into order upon the platform. In fact, no sooner were the third class carriages brought forward than a rush was made at the clumsy, uncovered, cattle-pen looking vehicles; it was in vain that the doors were set open – the eagerness of the crowd was far too great for such a sober mode of entrance; they climbed over the sides, or mounted the wheels affording no bad idea of their gallant countrymen storming a breach. How they contrived to manage, packed together so closely as they were, it is impossible to conceive.*

Between May and October 1851, Waterloo's capacity was tested further when crowds flocked to London to visit the Great Exhibition; the early exposition was situated in the vast 'Crystal Palace' based in Hyde Park. In a board meeting held shortly after the Great Exhibition had concluded, Chairman Lord Morley heaped praise upon the staff at Waterloo, saying they had 'exerted themselves to the utmost' throughout the five-month event.

In a further comment, which is perhaps rather telling as to the state of railways during the Victorian era, Lord Morley also asserted that it was 'under God's providence' that 'they had passed through the period without meeting with any fatal accident or without materially interfering with the ordinary traffic of the line'.

One person who likely disagreed with Lord Morley's latter statement was a correspondent to the *London Daily News*, who identified themselves simply as 'a daily passenger'.

Throughout the period of the Great Exhibition, the L&SWR had laid on extra trains, which, during quieter periods, led to some logistical problems due to the limited space at Waterloo. As the 'daily passenger' described:

> *…all these carriages, when not in use…have been suffered to stand upon and block one of the lines of rails for a considerable distance from the terminus, and it has therefore become necessary to run all the down trains on one line of rails.*

At one point this arrangement apparently led to a minor collision. The 'daily passenger' suggested a solution for Waterloo's limited capacity: that the L&SWR should invest the profit they had received from the Great Exhibition by expanding into the vacant ground beside the station (which the company had already purchased). He also suggested that such a move would pave the way for improving the 'beggarly wooden buildings of which the present terminus is composed, and which cannot in any case last many years'.

By 1852 the L&SWR were of the same opinion. At a meeting held in February of that year, it was announced that the temporary wooden buildings were both 'inconvenient' and 'insalubrious', and that it was therefore:

...the intention of all the directors to call for designs, under public competition, for a permanent building to comprise offices for the passenger and parcel traffic and...the general offices of the company. This building will be placed on the site of the Waterloo station, care being taken that the plan will be compatible with the future completion of Waterloo station, when the time may have arrived for undertaking that work.

The directors have found, from experience, that such permanent buildings can no longer be postponed consistently with the interests of the company, and the health of the persons in their employ.

Reading between the lines, the original makeshift buildings at Waterloo must have been shabby affairs by this point – it was even reported, by an officer from the Board of Health, that improvements to the station were required for the sake of the L&SWR's employees' well-being.

It is also worth remembering that in the 1850s, the Thames – located just moments from Waterloo – was growing filthier and more polluted by the day, a situation that culminated in the 'Great Stink' of 1858. It is safe to assume that the putrid stench from the river would have been noticeable at Waterloo as it wafted towards the platforms. This, combined with the shabby buildings, no doubt made for a rather unpleasant working environment!

WATERLOO BEGINS TO BLOOM

By 1852 it was clear that the government was not going to budge regarding their stance on forbidding railways to nudge further into central London. This resoluteness made the L&SWR's anticipated extension towards the Square Mile increasingly unlikely, leading them to sell the property they'd purchased near London Bridge. This situation also encouraged the L&SWR to push ahead with improvements at Waterloo, with a view to creating a grander, more permanent terminal.

England's Last Duel

On 19 October 1852, the telegraph office at Waterloo received an urgent wire from Windsor station (now Windsor & Eton Central) stating that 'three persons, supposed to be Frenchmen, and who it was believed had been engaged in a duel, were on their way to London by the express train.' These gentlemen were indeed French, and upon arrival at Waterloo the trio were arrested, where they were discovered to have 'two small swords, beautifully mounted, a pistol case, and a knife with some blood upon it' about their persons.

It transpired that the duel, which had occurred at Priest Hill near Windsor, was slugged out between former naval hero Frédéric Cournet, and revolutionary figure Emmanuel Barthélemy. Both men – both briefly referred to in Victor Hugo's epic story *Les Misérables* – were fugitives, and it appeared that their quarrel lay in the fact that Cournet had been spreading malicious rumours about Barthélemy's lover.

The duel was messy – one of the guns misfired twice – and it was Cournet who lost. As he lay dying in Windsor, Barthélemy and his two friends, who had assisted in the deed, fled the scene and boarded a train to Waterloo. When the case came to trial the three were found guilty of manslaughter and received six months each in prison.

Shortly after being freed, Barthélemy found himself embroiled in another argument that led to a fight, although this instance lacked the gentlemanly conduct of before. Again Barthélemy killed his opponent, but this time the law was not so kind to him, and he was executed before a huge crowd at Newgate gaol in 1855.

Work to improve the station was soon underway, and continued quietly in the background without any disruption to services. Having said that, carpenters employed on the project made a shocking discovery in November 1852 whilst renovating the old cloakroom. Here they found a box in a forgotten cupboard that was 'found to contain the body of a full female infant'. Tragically it was estimated that the child's corpse had lain undiscovered at the station for twelve months.

Sadly, such instances were not uncommon at major railway stations during this era, and the fact that they did occur can be viewed as an indictment of the social attitudes that prevailed during the Victorian era.

In the late summer of 1853 it was announced in a board meeting that the 'new booking offices and extension to the roof are nearly completed'. It was also reported that the station had acquired a 'stock of horses' along with vans and wagons for the purpose of goods deliveries.

Although passengers were now blessed with sturdier facilities, in a half-yearly meeting at the Assembly Rooms on York Road the question was raised about the lack of a new boardroom for the L&SWR's directors. Chairman John Hibbert said that he understood that the reason such a building did not yet exist was that 'the foundation was bad, and that there was a danger of those offices, if they were built, sinking in'.

It was also suggested that the price they had been quoted was too high, and that a cheaper estimate was being sought. In summary, Hibbert said that 'although additional accommodation was much called for, some of the officers of the company were obliged to live in a filthy hot hole for some time longer'.

By early 1855 the board had acquired their new headquarters, it being reported in *The Times* on 16 February that the half-yearly general meeting 'was held yesterday at the company's new rooms at Waterloo-bridge station'. At this meeting, the subject of the 'West End of London & Crystal Palace Railway' (the WEL&CPR) was raised.

The Neighbour that Never Was

In June the previous year, the Crystal Palace that had been used to stage 1851's Great Exhibition had been rebuilt in Sydenham as part of a large leisure complex. It was the aim of the WEL&CPR to provide this enticing site with a rail link from central London. The company had ambitions of merging their line with the L&SWR, and terminating it at a new station built on a vacant plot beside Waterloo's north-western side.

At the 1855 meeting, however, the WEL&CPR's request to occupy this space was refused, the explanation being that 'it was thought that in the general improvement and development of railways the company would require it for their own purposes', a view that soon proved valid.

The WEL&CPR ended up being a short-lived enterprise that was eventually purchased outright by the London & Brighton South Coast Railway. The original line only stretched as far as Battersea Wharf, although its creation would go some way to paving the way for Victoria station.

FURTHER EXPANSION

On 13 July 1855 a special meeting was held at Waterloo's new boardroom, where it was proposed that a bill should be presented to parliament in the hope of gaining assent to build various expansions (this bill would become known as the South Western Railway Capital & Works Act). The bill requested powers to improve and extend the Nine Elms depot – which included constructing a line across Nine Elms Lane to link up with a proposed wharf on the Thames – raising money to purchase land, and to 'improve the approach to Waterloo station'.

Intriguing for the time was the report describing this meeting, which noted that it 'was numerously attended, and was graced with the presence of a lady, an unusual circumstance at a railway meeting.'

The bill was given the go-ahead, and the works were successful: the crossing of Nine Elms Lane sowed the seeds for what would become the huge Brunswick Yard development, a sprawling area of tracks, cranes and offices, which formed the northern counterpart to Nine Elms goods depot. Brunswick Yard looks very different today, however, the area being covered by the St George's Wharf complex.

It was reported in a board meeting of August 1860 that the other works around Waterloo – described as 'work of absolute necessity considering the increased traffic' – were complete. They included widening the

What Lies Beneath…

Due to its elevated position, the expansion at Waterloo necessitated the construction of more arches, adding to the many that had been built in the 1840s. Today these structures remain beneath the tracks, platforms and concourse, forming a vast, eerie labyrinth.

Currently this area is mostly empty, although this wasn't always the case. Until relatively recently, the arches provided useful accommodation for various offices, clubs and other facilities used by railway staff. The derelict remains of these units are still in place, lurking beneath the feet of the millions of commuters who pass through the station every year, completely oblivious to the secret world beneath them.

Amongst other things, the arches supporting Waterloo are home to a World War II air-raid shelter for staff, the remains of several drinking establishments – including one used by British Transport Police until the 1990s – a typing pool, complete with an elevated office overlooking the area, ominous graffiti, vintage signs, antique lavatories (very few of which were designated for female employees) and several bathtubs, which could be booked by staff requiring a dip.

Arch beneath Waterloo.

Abandoned bathtub beneath Waterloo.

Old signs beneath Waterloo.

Derelict lavatory beneath Waterloo.

A dusty, full-sized snooker table remains in situ, as does a boxing ring and the remains of a shooting gallery provided for staff who were members of a popular rifle club. Nowadays of course the idea of providing gun facilities within the confines of a national railway hub sounds unthinkable, although the gallery beneath Waterloo remained in use until at least the 1980s.

Abandoned snooker table beneath Waterloo.

Archaic sign beneath Waterloo.

Office and typing pool beneath Waterloo.

arches and erecting new booking offices, the total cost of which amounted to £23,397. This work was carried out by Messrs Nicholson & Sons, who were based on High Street, Wandsworth. Following the completion of the project, this construction company had a substantial surplus of material left over, namely:

8,000 white and yellow battens, 4,000 deals, 130 loads of timber in scantling, 18,000 feet die square stuff, scaffolding, wheeling planks, a quantity of firewood principals, joints, slates &c.

This large collection of miscellaneous items was auctioned off on 6 March 1860, outside Waterloo on York Road.

Although much needed, the 1850s expansion work still wasn't enough, as Waterloo's popularity continued to increase, placing the facilities under further strain. On 9 June 1859, shortly before the improvements were complete, a writer to *The Times*, referring to themselves simply as 'A Sufferer', penned an account of the state of the station at the time that was inspired by personal experience:

Sir, The wretchedly unsafe condition of the Waterloo station of the South-Western Railway forces me, a frequent but most reluctant passenger on the line, to appeal to you against the unjustifiable neglect of the directors.

The station is not nearly half large enough for the traffic there, and the consequences of all sorts, and constant danger to life and limb, of which those who have not experienced it cannot form a notion, and those who once have will never expose themselves to it again if they can help it.

The platforms are not nearly large enough for passengers without any luggage, and with the luggage on them, nothing but the constant careful warning of the inspectors and other officials prevents ladies and children, and even men, from being forced among the wheels of the carriages.

The rails are so close together that it is often necessary to move two whole trains in order to use a turntable for a single carriage; and the rails are so few that trains have to wait down the line till others are got from under the shed.

The cabstand is so miserably small and so badly arranged that it sometimes takes 20 minutes to get a cab, and it constantly happens that in order to get to one, ladies and children have to be dragged among the horses and wheels, to their no slight terror and danger.

Most earnestly do I, who cannot help myself, entreat all those travellers and excursionists who can travel by any other line to do so, and to spare us the infliction of their addition to the crowding and confusion which we are doomed to suffer…

The following month, a similar view was provided by a journalist reporting on crowds attempting to travel to a National Rifle Association event at Wimbledon:

At the Waterloo station there was again a crush, confusion, and a succession of very bad quarter hours to be passed by the public before they could disburse their cash for tickets.

The impediments the railway authorities put in the way of those who come to them more in hand are sometimes singularly perverse; but with a week's practice the difficulties were brought to perfection on Saturday at the Waterloo station.

Every 'one and return' is fixed at a sum that in nine cases out of ten requires change to be given from two shillings or half-a-crown; and one clerk at one small window was the receiver and payer for the whole rush. With the least foresight and arrangement these scenes of mobbing and scrambling, disagreeable to the strong, and really dangerous to the weak, might be avoided…

WATERLOO'S WINDSOR STATION

Event days aside, the overcrowding of Waterloo was primarily due to its being a commuter hub. It was for this reason that, as part of the expansion, new platforms were added to Waterloo's north-western

Waterloo station, viewed from Waterloo Road c.1900.

side for the purpose of dealing with local traffic – that is, the lines to Richmond, Windsor and Reading, and the 'loop line' to Hounslow. These platforms essentially formed a new, separate terminal, which became known as 'Windsor station' (and later, 'North station'), complete with its own booking office, cab stand, waiting rooms and so on. *The Surrey Gazette* provided a detailed view of this facility as it appeared when new:

To obviate this difficulty [overcrowding on the suburban lines], the company have erected a new station near to the present one, and the approach to it is from the Waterloo-road. By these improvements the passenger traffic on the Richmond, Windsor, Reading and the Hounslow lines will be entirely separated from the present Waterloo station, both as to booking from and returning to London.

The buildings connected with the new stations are booking offices for the first, second and third class passengers, with waiting rooms. Four additional lines of rail and four extra platforms are put down, namely, two platforms to each pair of rails. The down and up lines are entirely new from the new station to the Falcon Junction [now Clapham Junction], where the Southampton or main line down trains run to the left.

At this junction the trains for Richmond, Windsor, Reading and the intermediate stations on the Windsor line diverge to the right. By this arrangement the Southampton up trains will no longer cross the Windsor line at the Falcon Junction, as has hitherto been the practice, an independent up line also being provided for the main line trains.

These improvements will much facilitate operations on the South-Western Railway, and prove a great convenience to the public. The new station was opened on Friday last, and all passengers for Richmond, Windsor, and Reading, as well as by the Loop line, are now required to book at the new station.

The new terminal would have been deemed especially necessary as the L&SWR were extending a long-distance line to Exeter, an inter-city link that required the use of Waterloo's original platforms. This new route was officially opened on 18 July 1860 when a group of directors from the L&SWR, accompanied by members of parliament and other VIPs, departed Waterloo in a dozen first-class carriages at eight o'clock in the morning. The journey took seven hours, with the train pulling into Exeter at 3pm sharp.

In terms of pedestrian access, the Windsor station would not be fully connected to Waterloo's mainline platforms until 1880, when a much needed footbridge was constructed. Prior to this, travellers were required to take a lengthy detour, dodging numerous carts and vehicles on the crowded roadway.

HARD TIMES

Despite Waterloo's importance, many passengers bound for the station were inconvenienced by a toll that required payment on Waterloo Bridge – as described in *The Graphic* in 1872:

Nearly one million persons are annually arrested at the gates with a demand for a toll. Many of these are in vehicles; and perhaps some of our readers may know what it is to be pulled up at a narrow entrance when in a hurry to catch a train at the Waterloo station, or be stopped behind a file of cabs while a gentleman in a Hansom is fumbling in his pockets for a couple of coppers. Then there is for foot-passengers the inevitable collector who compels them at both ends to push their way through a stiff turnstile…

As well as providing an obstacle to those in a rush, it was also believed the cost of crossing the Thames was having a detrimental effect on the development of the area around Waterloo. As one report from autumn 1872 suggested:

If the visitor still has doubts, let him come down to the vicinity of the Waterloo station, and he will find the district is not improving as it ought, and that rents, in fact, are largely kept up by the letting of houses for immoral purposes.

In short, Waterloo during this period was blighted by extreme levels of poverty, perhaps best summed up – also in 1872 – by the Reverend Mr Richardson who, speaking on behalf of the Church Pastoral Aid Society, declared:

...if there was a vile piece of London, it was there... In this poor neighbourhood gin palaces flourished...There was not one poor family in the district that could produce a set of tea things or a whole set of crockery ware.

The toll on Waterloo Bridge was finally lifted after sixty years in 1878, when its management was taken over by the Metropolitan Board of Works. Although this did appear to improve much of the area, pockets of crippling poverty still existed around the terminal. Charles Booth's late nineteenth-century poverty map displays a true mixture of social classes in the

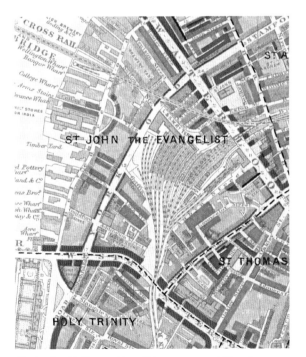

Charles Booth's Poverty Map of the area around Waterloo.

area, from the 'well-to-do' along York Road, to 'semi-criminal' on both the north-eastern side of Waterloo Road and a portion between modern-day Upper Marsh and Station Approach.

One telling news item from this era described a 'gang of roughs who infest the neighbourhood of the Waterloo station', who were brazen enough to beat a police constable close to death. Conditions for those who relied upon Waterloo for work were far from perfect, too.

In the 1870s, the Cabmen's Shelter Fund – famous for establishing the distinctive green dining huts around London that are still used by taxi drivers today – arranged for a petition asking that they might establish a larger shelter within Waterloo.

By this point, the terminal boasted the capital's largest cab rank – often stretching for a quarter of a mile – and the sheer number of cabbies meant that the existing facilities were '...quite inadequate to accommodate one quarter of the men who frequent the station...and are compelled to go either to some distant coffee-house, or, more often it is feared, to the gin palace.'

In the days when road vehicles were horse drawn and their drivers exposed to the elements, finding decent shelter was indeed a pressing concern. In the particularly severe winter of 1895, a number of cab and omnibus drivers perished from hypothermia whilst at work. This included one poor soul, a Covent Garden porter, who was discovered '...dead in a cart outside Waterloo station, death having resulted from exposure to the severe frost. The man's hair was covered with ice...'

It wasn't only humans who faced hardship at Waterloo. The slopes leading up to the terminal's concourse were viciously steep, meaning that the horses charged with hauling cabs, vans and omnibuses were placed under horrendous strain. In the nineteenth century these notorious inclines sparked a number of incidents, such as the following, which occurred in January 1895:

Shortly before 5 o'clock on Saturday afternoon a terrible accident took place at the departure side of Waterloo station, resulting in the death of a man and fearful injuries to a woman.

It appeared that at the time in question a man in the employ of the G.P.O drove a pair of horses up the incline leading from Waterloo Road. On nearing the steps the driver turned the pair-horse van, and the animals immediately dashed down the incline leading to Griffin-Street, York Road. The driver was hurled from his seat, and both wheels passed over him. A lady was also knocked down, and the near wheel passed over her leg.

The terrible conditions under which horses were expected to work at Waterloo gave rise to considerable concern amongst the public. As one commentator noted in 1880, 'the incline between Waterloo Bridge and Waterloo station is very great', yet single-horse omnibuses 'in which the animal is sorely overtaxed' were expected to contend with the steep ramp all day and every day. The same writer noted that countryside folk were often fined for subjecting their horses to far less.

One of the most heartbreaking illustrations of working horses at Waterloo was provided in this letter to *The Globe* dated 28 January 1898:

Sir – outside Waterloo station this morning at 10 a.m. was an instructive sight. Over a dozen Post Office vans, labelled 'Royal Mail', were waiting on the slope leading down to York Road. The horses were a disgrace to any cat's meat man – let alone a Government Department – heads hanging down and ribs protruding…

The writer went on to announce that such a sight was a disgrace to humanity and, considering Waterloo was by now a major international gateway to London thanks to its link with Southampton docks, an embarrassment to the nation.

Waterloo–Baker Street omnibus, which operated in the late nineteenth and early twentieth centuries, now kept in the London Transport Museum Depot, Acton.

Waterloo Beasts

Throughout the nineteenth century, Waterloo received an intriguing number of animal passengers. In May 1877, for example, it was reported that a live 26lb salmon, en route to the recently opened Westminster Aquarium, was brought in.

Even bigger, however, in the same year, was a 9ft 6in long Beluga whale, the unfortunate creature having been transferred by ship from New York after a stint on show at Coney Island. Upon arrival at Southampton, the whale was conveyed by the L&SWR in an open truck to London. The 'whale was then taken in a van from Waterloo station to the Aquarium' where it reportedly took a dozen labourers to lift him into his tank.

By 1895 the L&SWR was adept at handling exotic creatures. That year, a giraffe was procured for London Zoo. On the voyage, the creature was kept on deck, but when it came to the railway journey from Southampton to London, the giraffe's tall neck posed a problem due to the number of tunnels and bridges. To counteract this, a collapsible box was devised, which apparently forced the giraffe to lower its head from 12ft to 8ft. As reported, 'this cleared the railway arches, and it was safely delivered at Waterloo station, whence it was taken on a lorry to the Gardens.'

More straightforward was a cow, which, in October 1881, was brought into Waterloo with the order that it was 'to be left till called for'. After some time, Waterloo porter Charles Watts took it upon himself to walk the beast all the way from the station to Muswell Hill. For his troubles, Charles found himself fined ten shillings for the heinous crime of 'moving a cow out of the metropolis without an order'.

Less fortunate were the many turtles that passed through Waterloo over the years in order to satisfy the Victorians' predilection for turtle soup. The arrival of these creatures often provided a source of fascination and was reported in the press numerous times. This description comes from September 1898:

> Passengers who alighted at No. 4 platform of the main line were surprised to see several large animals lying on their backs on a quantity of straw. Upon the shells which covered them were black paint marks – initials and figures. The strange creatures were a consignment of turtles from the West Indies… They were all alive and had been placed on their backs to prevent their moving. In all there were about 60 of the turtles. They will be kept in water tanks until the time comes for them to be killed.

SOUTH STATION

In 1873 the L&SWR produced a bill requesting permission to extend Waterloo's north-western side and to realign roads beneath the station, namely the now vanished Vine Street and Cross Street. More crucially, however, the bill also sought to widen the terminal's south-eastern side. After agreeing to the Metropolitan Board of Works' caveat that any new arches over the streets had to be at least 40ft (12m) wide, this expansion was given the go-ahead.

By 1876 construction of what would become known as 'South station' (occasionally referred to in the press at the time as 'New Waterloo') was under way. Like Windsor station, this terminal within a terminal was granted its own platforms, booking offices and other facilities. Its purpose was to alleviate pressure by serving suburban stations located on the longer distance mainline.

On Sundays South station was closed, with services instead running from Waterloo's original platforms, which, due to the addition of Windsor and South stations was now termed 'Central station'.

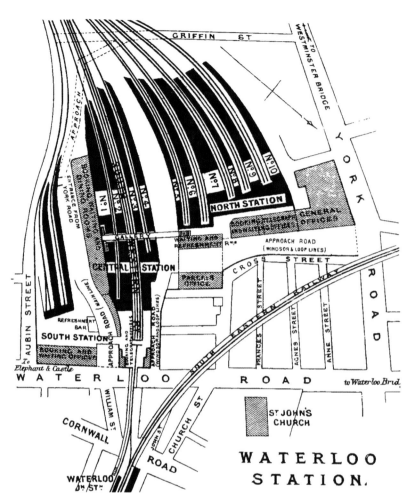

Map of Waterloo, 1888.

As its name suggests, South station was located on Waterloo's southern border, tucked between Central station and a lost road called Aubin Street. Its approximate footprint is now covered by present-day platforms 1 to 4. It was designed by the L&SWR's chief engineer, W. Jacomb Hood, and was 1,000ft (300m) long with a frontage of 160ft (50m). Upon opening, *The South London Press* provided the following description:

The substructure consists of brick arches, the foundations of which were sunk 15ft into the peat beds below. A light handsome roof of iron, wood, and glass, supported by iron columns, shelters the station from end to end and there are two platforms of considerable length. That in the middle is 750ft long, with an average width of 23ft, while the subsidiary platform is 450ft in length and 11ft wide.

The offices face the Waterloo Road and compromise an elegant building, partly in the Italian and Gothic styles, carried upon iron columns over the roadway in front of the entrance steps.

A spacious staircase leads from the street level to the reception platform which, 150ft long and 60ft wide, is immediately opposite the booking office and waiting-rooms. These latter are fitted with every regard to the comfort of the public, the sanitary arrangements, which are by Messrs Jennings of Stangate, being of the most improved description.

Site of the former South station.

South station was connected to its central counterpart by a footbridge, and the roadway's incline was made less severe than the other approaches to Waterloo, no doubt to the relief of London's hard-working horses. The platforms were laid with granite rock asphalt, and a hydraulic luggage lift was installed by W. Armstrong and Co. of Newcastle.

Another innovation at South station were the electrical indicators, displayed in two units for each platform road. These were intended to inform staff where the next outgoing train was bound for, and

took the form of boxes, inside which were six letters denoting:

H for Hampton Court
L for Leatherhead
K for Kingston via Malden
G for Guildford
S for Shepperton
O for leaving empty

Depending on which train was heading out, the corresponding code would twist around. This system was operated via Waterloo's large A signal cabin, located just outside the terminal. With the expansion of tracks and the addition of South station, it became necessary to expand the A cabin, a task that was achieved without any disruption to traffic.

Waterloo's late nineteenth-century signal box had come a long way since the 'crow's nest' of the 1840s. Located approximately above present-day Leake Street, the expanded cabin bridged all the lines. It contained two storeys: the upper level being 60ft (18m) long by 30ft (9m) wide, and the lower 74ft (23m) by 30ft (9m). It accommodated some 130 levers,

Inside the A signal cabin, 1907.

and with a mess room and telephone room, was the world's largest signal box at the time.

THE UNFORTUNATE FATE OF SIR FRANCIS GOLDSMID

Throughout the nineteenth century, accidents resulting in the deaths of both passengers and railway employees were a relatively frequent occurrence. However, in May 1878, one such fatality received much attention and generated considerable debate as to the shortcomings of railway safety. The reason for this increased interest was that the victim happened to be Sir Francis Goldsmid, the Liberal Party MP for Reading.

Sir Francis Goldsmid.

Sir Goldsmid's life had been an impressive one. After studying law he was called to the bar in 1833, making him the first Jewish person to qualify as an English barrister. He entered politics in 1860 and became a generous philanthropist, supporting numerous Jewish charities as well as fighting to improve conditions for Jews living abroad.

On the evening of 3 May 1878, Sir Goldsmid arrived at Waterloo and as he attempted to disembark, slipped between the platform and the carriage's footboards. His injuries were most grievous: several ribs were broken, his pelvis was smashed and his legs crushed. The MP was rushed to nearby St Thomas's Hospital but he died less than an hour later. As he lay injured, Sir Goldsmid was supposedly heard to say he was pleased he'd been taken to a hospital of which he was a governor, before muttering his last words: 'Do not disturb me; let me die in peace.'

There was some confusion as to how Sir Goldsmid had managed to fall. What was certain was that the train had not come to a complete halt, but what was not clear was if he had been stepping down from the train intentionally before it stopped (as seen with many impatient commuters in the days of slam-door trains), or if he'd been led to believe the train had come to a halt; the theory behind this being that Waterloo's porters would often walk along trains as they rolled in, throwing the doors open looking for passengers to assist.

The ensuing debate about Sir Goldsmid's death exposed some revealing details about the state of Victorian railway infrastructure. One writer to *The London Evening Standard* claimed it was often necessary to climb – 'no other words will do' – or jump in and out of carriages. The writer also pointed out that the height between the floorboards and platforms on the L&SWR was often two to three feet, and for this reason they were aware of at least one person who 'being lame' avoided travelling on the L&SWR altogether.

The inquest into Sir Goldsmid's death also provided a telling description of the platforms at Waterloo as they existed in the 1870s:

The height [between the platforms and carriage footboards] at the Waterloo station varied between seventeen and thirty-one inches, these two heights corresponding pretty closely to those of a dining room chair and a dining room table, and it is certainly a reprehensible thing for a railway company to expect passengers to make a plunge of this kind, but unfortunately it has at present to be done.

When a train has apparently stopped there is often a jar backwards after a second or two, and the unwary traveller who is caught by it in descent of this considerable height runs great risk of a very awkward fall, if not to sharing a similar sad fate of the late member for Reading.

Captain Daniel Warren

Sir Francis Goldsmid wasn't the only high-profile figure to be killed in an accident at Waterloo in the 1870s. Just over a year previously, in February 1877, seventy-nine-year-old Captain Daniel Warren, who had been one of the L&SWR's longest serving directors, was knocked down by a train whilst crossing a set of tracks. As he lay dying, Captain Warren was heard to lament: 'It is strange that after cautioning people employed on the line during the thirty years I have been a railway director, that I should at last be killed by my own line…'.

LET THERE BE LIGHT

In February 1881 the L&SWR's directors announced they had decided to give electrical lighting a three-month trial at Waterloo, thus making the terminal one of the earliest locations in London to employ the new technology. The section of Waterloo selected for the experiment was South station. This choice disappointed *The South London Press*, who believed North station would benefit more, mainly because it would throw light upon 'the objectionable characters that nightly frequent it'.

Power was provided by the Brush Company, a US manufacturer of electrical generators founded by Charles Francis Brush in Cleveland, Ohio, in 1849. The company established itself in London in 1880, opening an office on Hatton Garden and a generator plant on Belvedere Road, a short distance from

Waterloo. The revolutionary new form of lighting, which was initially provided by fifteen lamps, was switched on in the presence of various officials at 5.40pm on Monday 7 February.

Within just a few days, and with quintessential British pessimism, one fellow wrote to *The Kilburn Times* to express how unimpressed he was with the newfangled illuminations. After describing how they were in a 'flickering state', cutting out about twice every five minutes, the writer declared that 'electric light will hardly win its way to popular favour if it is everywhere as badly looked after as at Waterloo station.'

On 6 March 1884 another experiment in electrical lighting was conducted, this time in a moving carriage on the 4.55pm Waterloo to Bournemouth service. The test was successful, although it required a hefty battery weighing 2cwt (100kg) to achieve. The battery reportedly held twenty hours' worth of power, and was said to provide sufficient light that the small print of a newspaper could be read without any strain.

A COMPENDIUM OF CHAOS

By the 1880s Waterloo station was, to put it mildly, a complete mess. It now consisted of three separate terminals, each with its own entrance, cab rank, booking office, refreshment room and telegram office, and there was no attempt to consolidate them. Bizarrely, in what today would be deemed a health and safety nightmare, there was even a set of tracks laid across the main pedestrian concourse, the purpose of which was to link the terminus with Waterloo junction (*see* Chapter 5).

To make matters worse, passengers struggling to find their way around the three terminals were guided by misleading signage. Even more baffling were the platforms, which were numbered in a confusing manner – or, in the case of South station, not at all!

To add to the headache, the smaller stations went by various colloquial names, inspired by political events of the period. North station (aka Windsor station) was dubbed 'Khartoum'. South station was sometimes called Suburban station or, in a similarly bombastic fashion to its northern counterpart, 'Cyprus'. It is not surprising, therefore, that the situation at Waterloo attracted frequent criticism and derision.

The most famous and oft-quoted example of this occurs in Jerome K. Jerome's humorous 1889 novel, *Three Men in a Boat*, in which it is said: 'Nobody at Waterloo ever does know where a train is going to start from, or when it does start, is going to, or anything about it…'.

There were also many normal, everyday commuters who would frequently write to the press to air their grievances. This was often done under the guise of quirky pseudonyms – not unlike many of today's railway users who besiege the social media with accounts of the railway companies they are forced to suffer.

Many of these Victorian complaints have much in common, and it is worth quoting some of them here at length in order to gain a real taste of just how frustrating nineteenth-century Waterloo could be. In January 1881, for example, we have a 'Seething Wells' who describes the perils of the morning rush hour:

> The traveller arrives by the 9.16 train from Surbiton upon a narrow and dangerous platform, crowded with hurrying passengers, officials, and porters either obtrusively rough or carelessly obstructive. Soldiers' baggage, milk cans, fish, and vegetables separate him from the cab which he seeks by a narrow space which he is forbidden to cross, and by a dangerous walk of some hundreds of yards, which he is compelled to take instead.

Seething Wells did offer a rare degree of understanding, however, suggesting that the reason 'this station should have been constructed to combine the maximum discomfort and inconvenience to passengers' was 'owing perhaps in some measure to geographical facts'.

Seething Wells' depiction of Waterloo as a crowded, turbulent place was echoed by others. One correspondent writing to *The Globe* in January 1885 described the terminal as a 'rabbit burrow', whilst another, calling themselves 'Traveller', compared the place to a 'bear garden'. Another likened Waterloo to a 'dark cavern'.

During this period, the most notorious aspect of Waterloo was the difficulty in locating one's required platform. In October 1883, a journalist from *The Sporting Life* stated 'Waterloo station ranks second only to Hampton Court Maze', adding that 'the ordinary traveler should always allow himself ten minutes to find from which platform his train is to start'.

Another journalist, reporting for *The Islington Gazette* in August 1897, declared Waterloo to be 'the most complex puzzle the world ever saw', before proceeding to describe a recent experience:

> On this occasion the playful practical joke of the managers was – Where to find the twelve o'clock train to Hampton Court. It is reputed to go from the South station, but the man there said, as he mopped himself, that it went from No. 1 mainline. At No 1 mainline they said it went from the south, but after a hot argument with an official, a deviation was made in favour of mainline No 2.
>
> There, an official giant, with a chimney-pot hat, declared in favour of No. 1, but the number was filed by a train for South Africa, which melted me even to look upon.
>
> Ultimately, at 20 minutes past 12, the 12 o'clock train did go from No 1, and a startled porter said, 'Well, I'm blowed!'

Some accounts of the difficulties experienced at Waterloo were so convoluted they would likely be deemed 'Kafkaesque' today. Take this example, written by 'J.C.' to *The Times* in the 1890s:

> I arrived at Waterloo station with my two daughters, whom I was about to see into the 11.5 train advertised in 'Bradshaw' to go to Surbiton…
>
> On reaching the main line entrance, the usual place of starting, we were received by a juvenile official in blue coat and buttons, who, after taking down our luggage, inquired if we were going to Surbiton, and on our answering

'Yes', replied, 'Then you have come to the wrong platform; you must go to the other side.'

The luggage was put up again, and we drove to the other side and found ourselves below the platform outside, the cabman saying he was not allowed to drive in.

We had our luggage taken down, but there were no porters to be had, so after waiting some time, I went back to the main entrance, and asked for a porter, when I was informed that we were at the right place at first, and ought not to have been sent away.

We therefore put up our luggage again, and drove back to the main entrance where we had at first alighted. A porter informed us that the 11.5 train went from the nearest platform to the entrance, and he labelled the luggage and deposited it there.

After waiting some time and seeing no train draw up, I asked another official from which platform the 11.5 train was to start, and he pointed to a platform beyond. I went there, and seeing a guard standing by inquired of him, and he said, 'Yes, that is the 11.5 train, but you cannot go by Surbiton by it, for it only stops there to pick up, not to set down.'

I asked also a porter, who confirmed this account. I then saw a ticket examiner looking at the tickets of the passengers in the train, and I asked him.

'Certainly, Sir,' he said, 'this train stops at Surbiton, and you can go by it.'

I therefore put my daughters into the train, and went back to the first platform in search of the luggage. There it was lying, but I could not get any porter to take it across. I spoke to several, but they made various excuses. There seems to be an understanding amongst railway porters that if one porter brings in some luggage, no other porter is to touch it.

In despair of getting my luggage across I went to the stationmaster's office and complained. A clerk came out with me and inquired why the luggage was not taken across; but as soon as he heard that it was for Surbiton, he said, 'This train does not go to Surbiton, Sir; we cannot allow you to travel by this train.'

I replied, 'The train is advertised to Surbiton, and the ladies, to whom this luggage belongs, are already in the train.'

He then appealed to a superior official who promptly gave judgment – 'certainly this train goes to Surbiton, Sir; certainly you can travel by this train.'

I then fortunately spied the original porter who had labelled the luggage, and asked him why he did not take it to the train. He answered, 'You told me you were going by the 11.5 train.'

He then took the luggage across just before the train moved out of the station with my two daughters…

As the train moved out I saw the inspector standing by, and told him my story. He answered, 'Why did you not speak to me, Sir? I could have put you right.'

In a similar vein is this letter, sent by a 'Season Ticket Holder' to the London Daily Mail in May 1896:

On Saturday last I arrived at Waterloo station shortly before twelve o'clock intending to travel by the 12.5 to Fulwell. On my arrival I noticed a light blue placard headed 'Kempton Park Races' on which it was announced that the ordinary trains to Fulwell, Hampton and Sunbury would not run between the hours of eleven and one, but no mention was made of the suspension of any other trains.

I then purposed to go down by the 12.20 to Teddington (via Richmond), but was informed that this also had been suspended, and that due notice of its suspension had been posted in the station.

After some little trouble I discovered a red placard announcing the suspension of this train, and I then crossed over to the South station with the view of proceeding by the 12.32 (via Wimbledon), this being a train which runs on Saturdays only, but found this had been suspended without any notice. I ultimately *travelled by the 1.5pm from Waterloo, which arrived at Teddington a quarter of an hour late.*

Again similar is this complaint, from a W. Domett-Stone to *The Times*, October 1894:

I have frequently been told in answer to the question, Which train for Wimbledon? 'Top, right hand side', to find myself with other passengers, after the lapse of a few minutes, obliged to change to a train in another part of the station.

This was just one of a slew of letters on the subject written to *The Times* in that same month. Other examples include an account from H. Stopes, who claimed: 'Waterloo is a name of dread, owing to the ignorance and want of courtesy of the bulk of officials.'

'A Daily Grumbler' meanwhile complained that Waterloo was essentially a free-for-all, with second- and third-class ticket holders often boarding first-class carriages without redress. The most caustic criticism of all, however, came from 'One of the Tired', who, upon arriving into Waterloo late, overheard 'an angered passenger ask one of the staff when the traffic manager is either going to die or retire.'

Less scathing, but still illustrative of the conditions at Waterloo, is this excerpt from a short story, *The True Story of a Businesslike Girl*, published in *The St James's Gazette* in December 1894:

There is ever a gay indecision, a diverting recklessness, about Waterloo station. Nobody knows on which platform a train is likely to arrive, and the law being tricky in regard to games of chance, it is only the very youthful porters who venture to guess. Thus it is that folk who want to meet a mild demure train from Surrey, suddenly find themselves faced by the important bustling Cape special from Southampton.

If the confused staff, overcrowded platforms and perplexing signs were not bad enough, it appears that even the station's timepieces were out to bamboozle the travelling public. Writing in May 1896, a 'Season Ticket Holder' described the 'eccentricity of the clocks at Waterloo station':

On my mentioning to one of the officials that the time of the clocks all differed, he informed me as an apology that they were made by different makers. On more than one occasion the principal clock was too fast, and the trains started, consequently, before their time. May I suggest that this company should adopt the now almost universal expedient of having their clocks synchronised, and thus save the passenger very unnecessary inconvenience?

This account of the station's difficulties appeared in April 1907:

The name Waterloo Station has hitherto been a synonym for confusion and irritability. Except to those who use this terminus frequently, its platforms are mystifying, and an ample margin of time is desirable to ensure finding the right one before the time of departure.

To reach the elevated station by cab is an experience not unmixed with excitement. From this eastern end your steed struggles up steep and slippery inclines and you would not be surprised to see your trunk and portmanteau slide off the roof of the vehicle and pirouette backwards into Waterloo Road.

From the western end you drive along insalubrious thoroughfares, then thread your way through tortuous tunnels, dark and damp, and finally climb up a mountainous bank. Coming away, when the steps are slippery with mud, the horse most likely puts out his front legs and slides to the bottom. It is always a relief to leave Waterloo station behind either coming or going...

CHAPTER 4

The Necropolis Railway

By the early nineteenth century London's graveyards were facing catastrophe. With the Industrial Revolution in full flow, the city's population had grown rapidly, which, bolstered by appalling poverty and abominable sanitation, meant that so too had the city's death rate. With the adoption of cremation as an accepted method of disposal still some decades off, London's burial sites – most of which were confined to small churchyards – were struggling to cope.

To address the issue, parliament passed a bill in 1832 encouraging larger, private cemeteries to be built. These burial grounds soon began to mushroom around what was then London's outer perimeter, starting with Kensal Green in 1833. This was followed by West Norwood in 1837, Highgate, Abney Park and Brompton in 1840, and Tower Hamlets in 1841.

A DESPERATE SITUATION

Despite the establishment of these larger cemeteries, London's smaller graveyards continued to cram in burials, piling coffins on top of each other in a process known as 'bedding up'. The situation deteriorated further in the 1840s when a cholera epidemic claimed the lives of over 10,000 Londoners. As an example of how desperate the situation had become, it was declared at a meeting held in September 1849 to discuss the overcrowding of St Botolph's Church, Bishopsgate, that 'in many cases there was just enough earth to hide the coffin and cover it from view'.

Across the river, the grimly named Cross Bones Graveyard on Redcross Way, Southwark, was described as being 'completely overcharged with dead' and was said to be in such a dreadful state that body parts could be seen poking through the thin layer of topsoil.

Elsewhere, at Spa Fields burial ground in Clerkenwell, it was reported in 1845 that thirty burials had taken place in a single day. Here, too, coffins lay in such shallow graves that they were barely covered. So bad was the state of Spa Fields that 'it was impossible for the inhabitants to live in their houses through the continual stench.' It was also revealed that gravediggers at Spa Fields were digging up and burning recently buried coffins and – it was alleged – body parts in a futile attempt to claw back space.

These were just three examples, but similar conditions were commonplace across the capital.

THE LONDON NECROPOLIS & NATIONAL MAUSOLEUM COMPANY

London Necropolis & National Mausoleum Company coat of arms.

It was in the midst of this crisis that the London Necropolis & National Mausoleum Company was formed by entrepreneurs Richard Broun and Richard Spry. Although its title was not officially shortened until 1927, the press would often refer to this business as the 'London Necropolis Company'; for simplicity, I shall refer to it as the LNC.

From the outset the LNC thought big, envisioning a vast cemetery, which they initially conceived capable of holding all of London's dead. As it was to be some distance outside the capital, the railway was to play a major and innovative role, with special funeral trains conveying the coffins directly from Waterloo.

A suitable site 27 miles (43km) south-west of London was identified at Brookwood, near Woking, on some 2,000 acres (810ha) of land belonging to the Earl of Onslow. The plot was dry and sandy, not suitable for agriculture, but perfect for burials.

In January 1850, a meeting to discuss the proposition of siting the Necropolis at Brookwood was held at the

Railway Hotel, Woking. At this gathering – said to be the largest ever held in the parish – locals were treated to a rousing speech by Sir Broun, who, in the face of what must have been a tough sell, explained that if they accepted the massive cemetery on their doorstep, the folk of Woking would be doing a proud civic duty:

The object of this company, as the name implies, is to furnish London with that which is at length felt by all classes of the community to be a great and crying desideratum – namely a 'CITY FOR THE DEAD' – at such a distance from the metropolis as public health requires; upon a scale of magnitude commensurate with a population rapidly increasing, which already exceeds 2,250,000 souls; at such charges as shall be consistent with the utmost possible economy; and at a site which will admit of spacious sepulchral structures, a NATIONAL MAUSOLEUM CHURCH, and variously decorated grounds, such as become not only the capital of the greatest and wealthiest nation in Christendom, but a people who for religious feeling, education, and general habits of life, hold the first rank among the believers of the Christian faith.

Broun added how inexplicable it was that such a 'repulsive system of burying the dead in intramural nooks and corners, in such grave-holes and charnel-dens as abound in London' had been permitted to develop, before going on to reveal the railway link:

The most desirable and perfect arrangements have been entered into with the directors of the London and South Western Railway for the reception and removal of the dead to the Necropolis, and for the conveyance and return of all classes of attendant mourners.

ESTABLISHING THE NECROPOLIS

The LNC gained traction in 1852 when the Burial Act came into force, forbidding any further burials within London's packed graveyards. In the same year, on 30 June, parliament passed a further Act permitting the creation of Brookwood Cemetery.

Ten weeks later, at 11.15am on 15 September, a special train left Waterloo carrying an estimated 250 to 300 'gentlemen, churchwardens, overseers, and others connected with the metropolitan parishes' for the thirty-minute ride to Brookwood, where they were set to inspect the 2,000-acre plot earmarked for the cemetery. Upon arrival, *The Globe* reported that the officials divided themselves into small knots before proceeding to examine the ground 'very minutely'. It was said that all were satisfied, and the article provided further details as to the cemetery's planned facilities.

As well as the necessary platforms for trains bearing coffins, it was also stated there would be reception rooms for arrivals and departures, stables, a manager's house, offices, a church (plus several auxiliary churches), a dissenters' chapel, an arched entrance, catacombs and even a hotel. Other reports mentioned how trains bound from a purpose-built facility at Waterloo would have the capacity to carry fifty coffins, along with fifty separate passenger compartments for the associated mourners.

Engineer William Cubitt was given the task of preparing the works and buildings required for the railway, which involved 'a piece of ground lying alongside the South-western Railway between Westminster and Waterloo bridges', an area today covered by Leake Street. Other work was conducted by Sydney Smirke and William Tite (Tite having designed the L&SWR's first Nine Elms terminal): these two individuals landscaped Brookwood and designed the relevant buildings there.

OPPOSITION TO FUNERAL TRAINS

Despite offering a clean, modern solution to London's burial problem, not everyone was in favour of funeral trains. The Bishop of London, Charles James Blomfield, for example, believed the speed and noise associated with railways would be an affront to the burial process. At a parliamentary debate to discuss the LNC bill in June 1852, he also voiced his opinion that London's burial crisis should be handled directly by the government, and 'entertained great doubts whether any private parties ought to be allowed to speculate in a traffic in the dead.'

William Cubitt.

Lord Shaftesbury.

In the same parliamentary debate, another of those opposed was the great philanthropist and social reformer, Anthony Ashley-Cooper, the 7th Earl of Shaftesbury (to whom the Shaftesbury Memorial Fountain – colloquially known as 'Eros' – on Piccadilly Circus is dedicated).

First, Lord Shaftesbury was against 'the great distance of the intended site from the metropolis'. For this view he was widely ridiculed, and told that 'from the Waterloo Station of the South-Western Railway the funeral trains could be conveyed in half an hour to the gates of the National Necropolis' – a time that was apparently quicker than the average horse-drawn funeral – 'to any one of the horrid intramural graveyards' within London. Reading between the lines, however, it could be argued that Shaftesbury feared that relatives would feel far removed from their departed loved ones.

Second, Shaftesbury challenged the LNC's calculations. In their projected targets, the company envisioned securing 'one-half, if not two-thirds of the corpses of persons dying in and about London'. Lord Shaftesbury claimed this figure was exaggerated, and that the LNC would have to secure '30,000 or 40,000 corpses annually' just to cover their preliminary expenses. He expressed further alarm in that

...he understood... the corpses were to be collected in great numbers, and were to be deposited in the dry arches under the Waterloo station, without any regard to decency, until it suited the railway company to convey them to the necropolis.

This was true, for in April 1854 the LNC had agreed to 'take the whole of the arches from the Waterloo station to the Westminster Road' as a repository for corpses, the aim of which was to keep the service separate from Waterloo's regular traffic.

Not surprisingly, this idea also generated hostility amongst local residents, who feared the health implications that this strategy would bring; this was mainly due to the theory of miasma – the widely held Victorian belief that disease was spread by foul smells. It was assumed that the storage of corpses

beneath Waterloo would 'produce an offensive and dangerous effluvia', especially in hot weather.

This opposition was expressed at a meeting where locals suggested the Nine Elms depot be used instead, as that locality was less populated. This idea was dismissed, however, as it was claimed that storing bodies within Waterloo's arches was perfectly safe, and that a move to Nine Elms would make the service less centralized.

Further protest came from traditional undertakers, who feared the LNC would put them out of business, an attitude that attracted attacks in the press. In January 1856, for example, an article in *The Lambeth and Southwark Advertiser* went to great pains to sing the praises of the LNC, before declaring:

The friends of the dead have, in the London Necropolis Company, a number of gentlemen who defend them from the extortion of undertakers.

The company undertake the whole business of a funeral at defined charges. You have only to post a letter enclosing a certain sum and you are free from all further care. The low class of undertakers, of course, oppose this company, but that is a reason why the public should patronise it.

Such criticism led some in the industry to strike back. In January 1859, one undertaker by the name of Autill was accused of libel when he claimed the LNC had the 'evil intention to do away with funerals together', accusing them of using Pickfords' vans to transport corpses not to Brookwood, but to nearby Woking Common, where they were dumped without ceremony. Fortunately for Autill the judge saw the humorous side of this, and threw the case out.

THE NECROPOLIS RAILWAY OPENS

Although granted parliamentary assent, work did not start immediately on the Necropolis railway due to dissensions amongst the board and delays in negotiations related to acquiring land. This meant that no preparations were conducted in 1853. When work did begin however, it was swift, with much of the construction of the Waterloo terminal being carried out between May and October 1854.

At Brookwood, around four miles (6km) of fencing was erected in order to enclose the initial 500 acres (200ha) of cemetery. Some 1,500 trees were planted, and a branch line (approximately three-quarters of a mile long), from the L&SWR's mainline, had its route through the cemetery's northern side and down towards the centre of the site. But for the first ten years, locomotives did not enter the cemetery – the carriages were instead hauled through the grounds by horses.

Two stations were built, south for Anglicans and north for Nonconformists and those of other religious beliefs.

On Tuesday 7 November 1854 Brookwood Cemetery was officially consecrated. At 12.30pm that day, a special train departed Waterloo carrying one hundred shareholders and other interested parties. The ceremony was conducted by Charles Sumner, the Bishop of Winchester – who did not travel by train, opting instead to ride in his private carriage from Farnham.

At the ceremony, the Act of Parliament from 1852 was read out, and three verses from the 39th psalm were sung. The process took little time, with the dignitaries back on board the train by 2.45pm; the return journey to Waterloo being

'accomplished...with the same ease and expedition as the down train'.

Following the consecration, the LNC opened for business on 13 November. Sadly, the first bodies booked on the service were a pair of stillborn twins, whose parents were a Mr and Mrs Hore of Ewer Street, Borough. The family were poor, meaning the parish of St Saviour's, Southwark, paid for the babies' funeral.

Charles Sumner, the Bishop of Winchester.

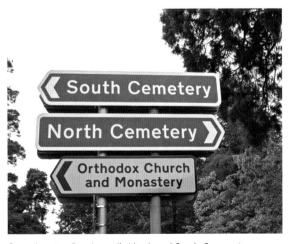

Signs denoting Brookwood's North and South Cemeteries.

Railway Avenue, path of the line through Brookwood.

THE LNC SETTLES IN

The buildings servicing the railway were rather more modest than the LNC's earlier vision, and there was no grand archway or hotel. At Brookwood, two 'neat mortuary chapels constructed in brick' had been built, one for the Church of England, and the other for dissenters.

In March 1855, Brookwood's two stations were granted licences to sell alcohol, making the cemetery the only one in the world to boast two bars. In the 1890s, these establishments were described as being boarded in 'bright white', and as such were the first thing to catch the eye of mourners as the train drew in. And it wasn't just mourners who drank there: both bars were popular with Brookwood's locals, who would often pop in for a snifter... and there are also numerous tales of the LNC's engine drivers imbibing a few too many whilst waiting for the return journey to Waterloo.

Back at Waterloo, the three-storey tall Necropolis station had been constructed at a cost of £23,231. The LNC usually referred to this as their 'Westminster Bridge station' – though some staff meanwhile preferred the nickname 'Corpse station' – and it was sited just outside the terminal, south of Waterloo's main buildings and close to the south-eastern end of Leake Street. The station had its own private access road, via which coffins could be delivered.

There was one platform and two sidings, which, like the main Waterloo terminus, were perched high up on arches. The platform was on the Necropolis station's highest level, and coffins were transferred to awaiting trains via a steam-powered lift.

The second floor contained waiting rooms, a workshop and board room (although the LNC also maintained offices a short distance away on Lancaster Place, just north of Waterloo Bridge), whilst the ground floor provided a grand entrance hall and staircase.

Shortly after the railway opened, the LNC held a board meeting in February 1855 at which the directors announced that 'the experiment of burial by railway has been found to work in a most satisfactory manner'.

In what appears to be an early example of market research, it was also stated that mourners were being asked if there was anything that could be done to improve upon their experience – and at that point customer satisfaction apparently stood at an impressive 100 per cent.

When the LNC first opened, those wishing to use the service were advised to give at least forty-eight hours' notice. Trains departed daily from Waterloo at 11.20am (sometimes given as 11.30am). As with conventional rail travel at the time, a number of classes were offered on the LNC, and these applied to both the living and the dead – corpses were even tagged with a one-way ticket.

1890s map depicting the site of the first Necropolis station, visible on the eastern side of the tracks.

SOUTHERN RAILWAY.

LONDON NECROPOLIS
COFFIN TICKET
WATERLOO to
BROOKWOOD
THIRD   CLASS

Third-class coffin ticket.

The LNC's pricing structure was considerably cheaper than that offered by traditional undertakers – in modern business parlance they would likely be labelled a 'disruptor'. The following is their price list, as published in November 1854:

First class: £21 14s 2d
Second class: £15 8s 2d
Third class: £11 10s 2d
Fourth class: £4 15s 2d
Fifth class, or walking funeral: £3 9s 2d

As a means of comparison, an undertakers named Sinclair and Son, operating in Finsbury around the same time, had their most expensive service priced at £28 10s.

The LNC's pricing structure included the cost of the undertaker, embalming, railway travel, a plot, and for the first three classes, a headstone and statue. Prices were based upon four mourners attending; should fewer or more be in attendance the price would be adjusted accordingly.

It was also possible for mourners to arrange for an independent undertaker to make arrangements and use the LNC just for the plot of land and transport to Brookwood. In this case, a first-class grave was charged at £2 10s.

The Necropolis Railway ran seven days a week, with Sundays on an amended timetable, its trains leaving fifteen minutes earlier than weekday trains, and taking one hour to complete the journey. Its undertakers were on call twenty-four hours a day.

Brookwood Cemetery South station platform. The building is a recent addition and forms part of a monastery.

Other LNC Services

As detailed, the LNC was spurred into existence by central London's massively overcrowded graveyards. Soon after Brookwood opened, many of the city's parishes therefore began to make arrangements with the company to have their graveyards exhumed and returned to acceptable levels.

Thus the remains of countless departed souls were dug up from many churches – including St Martin's-in-the-Fields, St Anne's (Soho) and St Pancras – and delivered to Waterloo for an LNC burial. Such re-internments happened on a regular basis. Even as late as 1903, the LNC removed 600 bodies from the former Wild Street Chapel, Drury Lane.

The LNC also sought to make a profit with other funeral paraphernalia. In 1857 they introduced funeral insurance, which allowed people to pay annual or monthly sums 'that will insure them a funeral, grand or humble, according to their payments'.

More intriguing was the development of biodegradable 'earth-to-earth coffins', which the company introduced in 1875. A brief report from *The Globe* on 3 December that year provides a vivid picture:

> *The London Necropolis Company has constructed some coffins upon a new system, the object of which is to hasten the dissolution of the body to its original elements more rapidly than can take place under the existing plan…*
>
> *The new coffins, which are constructed of compressed pulp held together with wooden fillets, present a similar appearance to ordinary coffins, and are just as substantial until they are put into the earth. The damp soon has an effect upon the pulp, which softens and falls away, leaving the earth to act upon the body.*

LNC earth-to-earth coffin.

By 1878 the LNC had gained a patent on the earth-to-earth coffin, and for any Victorian who was interested, examples were displayed in their offices on Lancaster Place and Kennington Road.

A DAY IN THE LIFE OF THE LNC

In February 1893, the *Pall Mall Gazette* published a perspicacious account of the Necropolis Railway when a journalist – known only as 'L.S' – was allowed to observe operations for a day. L.S began by describing the station as 'dingy and sombre, without being dilapidated, and is well upholstered and solidly furnished without being aggressively comfortable.'

Upon arrival at the station, L.S was given a tour. First was the mortuary, where around 300 ready-made coffins were stacked on standby for emergencies,

Illustration on a funeral train moving through Brookwood Cemetery.

the most common of which was the 'hotel death'. When such an incident occurred, LNC undertakers would go to the affected premises late at night with one of these coffins in order to avoid alarming other guests.

Throughout the day and night, L.S reported that between thirty and sixty bodies were brought to the mortuary, all ready for the following day's journey. The coffins were loaded by means of a lift, which could bear 'a score of coffins at a time'; this operation began at around 11am. The lift was hand operated 'by turning a great wheel', and was apparently conducted with 'painful slowness', with the operator 'stopping every now and again, with the twenty corpses overhead in mid-air, to doff his cap, to blow, to mop his brow, or to stretch his back.'

Once on the platform, the coffins were loaded on to shelves in the dedicated van, whilst mourners sat in their respective waiting rooms. On that day in 1893, the train on which L.S travelled held twenty-five corpses, all of which were third class.

The guard accompanying L.S was described as a 'fine, brown-bearded, open-faced man of forty-seven or forty-eight'. This character estimated that, in his eighteen years on the LNC, he had transported approximately 25,000 corpses. He also claimed the train was never crowded, and he had only ever had

to have a coffin in the brake van on one occasion, 'and that was a child's'.

When L.S questioned the guard as to whether working on the funeral service was monotonous, the guard replied:

Well, I don't know. I sometimes have a scene on the platform before we start. Perhaps the relatives quarrel over the will; perhaps, if the widower has been a bad husband to the wife he is about to bury, the womenfolk make things very lively for him, while perhaps it is the widow who has been bad to her husband, and who comes in for the bullying. Oh, there's lots of human nature to be seen on that platform, I tell you.

The guard also said he'd never had to carry bodies of those he knew in life, although 'my mates have sometimes had their own dead relatives in the train. It's been a hard time for them then, poor chaps.'

THE SECOND NECROPOLIS STATION

By the 1880s, Waterloo's expansion was threatening to engulf the LNC's station. The extension of the A signal box was now squeezed against the northern tip

Waterloo's A signal cabin – a wall belonging to the first
Necropolis station can be seen on the right.

of the LNC, necessitating the placement of a supporting pylon on the Necropolis railway's platform.
In return the L&SWR paid to have the Necropolis
station's entrance clad in white, glazed brick. There
was also a caveat that the LNC could request the
removal of the pylon at any time.

It soon became clear, however, that the Necropolis
station's location was most inconvenient, its existence making any expansion of Waterloo's approaches
impossible. It was therefore decided to demolish the
station and relocate.

When the time arrived, the LNC had a good hand:
their removal was key if the L&SWR wished to expand,
and due to the clause regarding the pylon mounted on
their platform, they could also make things very difficult
in terms of the signal box. Thanks to this position, the
LNC were able to secure favourable terms, and in May
1899 an agreement was signed between the two companies in which the L&SWR agreed to every demand.

One of the clauses allowed the LNC to lease a plot of
land from the L&SWR for a small rent in perpetuity.
This new location was on the southern side of Westminster Bridge Road, approximately 420ft (130m)
south of the original building.

The L&SWR granted the LNC control over the
design of the new Necropolis station, and agreed to
place no limit on the number of passengers permitted

Engines and Rolling Stock

Although the LNC owned their coffin cars outright,
the locomotives and mourners' carriages were
provided by the L&SWR, as were the drivers, fire-
men and guards. The original carriages (built by
renowned railway engineer Joseph Beattie) and
coffin cars lasted almost eighty years, until replace-
ments were sought in the early 1930s. Replacement stock consisted of three saloons – including
one formerly used by Queen Victoria – and were
sourced from Crewe.

The locomotive most associated with the LNC
was the Drummond M7 0-4-4 tank, built at the

Drummond M7 locomotive, the type used on the
Necropolis railway.

L&SWR's Nine Elms works. By 1901, trains were generally quite short, consisting of the engine, the
guard's van, one corpse carriage and one mourner's carriage.

Interestingly, in September 1932, *Railway Magazine* described a vintage carriage dumped unceremoni-
ously at the point where the Necropolis line branched off from the main approach to Waterloo. Believed to
date from the 1860s, this old car had had its wheels removed and was being used as a 'yard cabin'. The article
described the carriage as being 'of the primitive three-compartment type with straight sides, square windows
and panelling, and with two of the three old-fashioned oil-lamp cowls still adorning the nearly flat roof.'

The second Necropolis station, Westminster Bridge Road.

Necropolis station chapel.

to use it. To sweeten the deal further, the L&SWR paid £12,000 in compensation, and also consented to allow mourners free travel on any return service from Brookwood to either Clapham Junction, Vauxhall or Waterloo.

The new station building (which still exists today as Westminster Bridge House) was designed by Cyril Bazett Tubbs and took two years to construct, at a cost of £43,494. The original station remained in use until the work was complete. The new station contained its own chapel (a feature not included in its previous incarnation), which allowed mourners who could not travel to Brookwood to attend a service.

Shortly after it opened in early 1902, *The South London Chronicle* presented a detailed overview of the new premises:

> *The new building is entered by a handsome archway. Inside, the stairs, balustrades, and panelling are of the finest English oak, and the effect is rich and pleasing to a degree. On the ground floor is an enquiry office and waiting room.*
>
> *Upstairs is the General Office and Counting House, with the Manager's parlour opening out, and other offices. Ascending by a further flight of stairs to the Board Room (a most pleasant and luxurious room) we come to a light apartment, where draughtsmen are at work on the various plans and maps of the estate, and the private office of the estate agent,*

Necropolis station entrance.

LNC counting house inside Necropolis station.

Necropolis station glass-roofed yard.

Necropolis station waiting room.

Necropolis station platforms.

who has himself designed the buildings and railway station which form the subject of this article.

All the arrangements of the premises are so controlled as to ensure complete privacy for the funerals which take place from here. Directly the carriages pass through the archway they are beyond the public gaze, and the glass-roofed station yard, with its white tiled walls and rows of palms and bay trees, produces anything but a morbid effect.

Several mortuary chambers are provided on the ground level, and these are already providing a long-felt want in the city where deaths so often occur in hotels and lodgings, where it is impossible for the body to remain.

For funeral parties ample provision is made in the way of waiting rooms so that friends can assemble with as much comfort as in a private house. On the right-hand side of the platform is a most sumptuous private chapel, with a handsome oak catafalque in the centre, and oak stalls for clergy and congregation. In this a

coffin might lie in a certain degree of state until the time of burial.

As for the platform running into the premises, the funeral trains draw up alongside the waiting rooms, and mounters pass straight into the reserved carriages, and the train starts on its 40 minutes' journey to Woking.

No detail has been overlooked that could possibly assist in the quiet and decorous conduct of the funeral from the London Necropolis Station, and the arrangements are such that two or three funerals may travel by the same train without one party being conscious of the presence of the other.

The same report mentioned a luncheon that took place at the Dover Castle Hotel, Westminster Bridge Road, where Cyril Bazett Tubbs and other LNC officials were present to answer questions. Here, the Chairman of the Board, Edward Ford North, admitted that the LNC had been losing money for many years, but with an optimistic air he boldly announced that, as London's big seven cemeteries

Other Necropolis Railways

The LNC's Waterloo to Brookwood line is certainly the best remembered funeral railway. However, it was not alone, as its establishment inspired other companies to offer a similar service. Less documented is the Great Northern London Cemetery Company (GNLCC), established in 1855 to offer a funeral service from Kings Cross to a cemetery at Colney Hatch (now New Southgate Crematorium), which, at 150 acres (60ha), was much smaller than its Brookwood twin.

Like the LNC at Waterloo, the GNLCC had a separate, dedicated station just outside Kings Cross. Designed in the style of a gothic chapel, this building was located on Rufford Street (off York Way). Although funerals on the GNLCC were cheaper, services ran just twice a week and operations ceased at some point in the early 1870s.

In 1858 there was talk of constructing a funeral service for Birmingham after a delegation visited Brookwood. Although the idea was agreed to be beneficial, it appears no further action was taken on the matter.

On the other side of the world in Sydney, Australia, a Necropolis railway began operating in 1869. The mortuary station was on Regent Street, close to the city's Central station, and trains ran to Rookwood Cemetery.

Sydney's funeral service lasted until 1948. The ornate station was dismantled and rebuilt as All Saints Church in the Canberra suburb of Ainslie, where it can still be seen today.

were becoming full, 'the time of the Necropolis Company was coming'.

In 1904 *Railway Magazine* described Waterloo's new Necropolis terminal as 'perhaps... the most peaceful railway station in the three corners of the kingdom', adding, rather poetically:

> *Here, even the quiet subdued puffing of the engine seems almost sympathetic with the sorrow of its living freight.... One is forcibly reminded of the last great station on the railroad of life; of the final platform; of the completion of this world's journey. And thus this cemetery station preached sermons more effective than those of most parsons who stand in the pulpits of our land.*

LAST DAYS OF THE LNC

Although Brookwood Cemetery was the largest in the world during its heyday (and remains Britain's biggest today), and the LNC were Britain's largest undertakers, the company never achieved the lofty figures they'd set out to achieve (thus proving that Lord Shaftesbury's doubts were correct). There was, however, some increase in traffic after 1901 following the opening of a crematorium at Woking.

During World War I, large areas of Brookwood were allocated for those killed in battle. This included sites for both British and Commonwealth forces (of whom 1,600 were buried), and an area for 468 American personnel; this is the only American World War I burial site in Europe.

A special non-funeral service also ran twice a week for those wishing to visit the cemetery.

The Westminster Bridge Road station found itself at the centre of considerable drama in March 1929 when Dundee-born policeman David Ford, fell to his death there. This tragedy occurred in the early hours of the morning when a burglar alarm was sounded at a shop on Westminster Bridge Road, five doors away from the station.

A squad from Kennington police station was sent to investigate, and whilst examining the ground floor, heard the footsteps of two men dashing up a staircase. PC Ford gave chase, climbing up on to the rooftops in hot pursuit. One of the fugitives scrambled across the Necropolis station's glass roof, managing to slide down the other side. But when PC Ford attempted the

Rear view of the former Necropolis station.

Brookwood Cemetery, military section.

same route, the glass broke and he 'crashed headlong to the concrete yard 40ft beneath'. He was rushed to St Thomas's hospital but died shortly after.

It would be World War II that finally ended the Necropolis station's operations. During an air-raid on the night of 16–17 April 1941, the Westminster Bridge Road station was pounded by explosives, destroying infrastructure and rolling stock beyond repair. The service managed to limp on for a few more weeks by relocating to a platform at Waterloo itself, but on 11 May 1941, the funeral line to Brookwood was officially closed. The last recorded funeral carried by the service was that of a Chelsea pensioner named Edward Irish.

Despite the closure of the line, the bar in Brookwood's south station remained in service until the

Necropolis station blitz damage.

1960s. The LNC also continued to conduct funerals, although coffins were now conveyed by road. The company finally folded in 1975.

In Britain, coffins continued to be carried by rail until the 1980s. This included two state funerals – that of Sir Winston Churchill in 1965, and Earl Mountbatten in 1979, both of which departed from Waterloo (*see* Chapter 9). As of writing, the last UK funeral service to be carried by rail was that of trade unionist Jimmy Knapp, whose coffin was transported from Euston to Glasgow in August 2001.

Approximate site of Brookwood Cemetery North station.

Bricks marking the former track at Brookwood.

CHAPTER 5

Waterloo East

In February 1901, an article entitled 'Some Little Known Railway Stations' by York Howell appeared in *The Railway Magazine.* The piece included several sites associated with Waterloo: the original Nine Elms terminus, the Necropolis station, and Waterloo Junction – now known as Waterloo East, having been renamed in 1977.

According to Howell, many rail users at the time had no idea Waterloo Junction even existed, or if they were aware, would struggle to pinpoint its location. His description still resonates today:

Although the folks who planned Waterloo Junction evidently set out with the deliberate purpose of making it as accessible as possible for travellers arriving at Waterloo to get at, they hardly succeeded.

For unless you are conversant with the high-level entrance, if you leave Waterloo Station by the main entrance, to reach the junction station, you must cross the high road and pass into a side street by the railway bridge…

You had better next ask somebody which is the turning to take, or you may find yourself streets away from where the entrance looms upon a narrow, dirty side-road, where no mortal Englishman would ever expect a railway entrance to an important station to be.

Waterloo East sign.

Looking towards Waterloo main from Waterloo East.

ORIGINS

As detailed in Chapter 1, the L&SWR's original terminal was established at Nine Elms, a considerable distance from central London. This situation was mirrored on the opposite side of town by the South Eastern Railway (SER), which was founded in 1836 to create a line between London and Dover.

The SER's terminal, opened in 1844, was situated in Bermondsey, at Bricklayer's Arms, parallel to the Old Kent Road and with its façade facing Pages Walk. Designed by Lewis Cubitt, this long-demolished building could be considered a prototype for the architect's later and better known work, Kings Cross station.

Like Nine Elms, Bricklayer's Arms sat at what was then a remote spot. The reason for this choice of location was that the SER did not wish to share London Bridge station and its approaches with the capital's oldest line, the L&GR, who had demanded high fees for such an arrangement. Therefore when the L&SWR began making plans to extend from Nine Elms to Waterloo, the SER's board took notice. In the mid-1840s they formulated a plan to further their line also, with a view to joining the L&SWR at Waterloo. The scheme was detailed in a booklet, circulated in January 1846:

> *The object... is to form a West End terminus for all the lines in connexion with the South-Eastern. This terminus will be formed, opening on the Waterloo-road, and also on the York Road, Lambeth, which will bring it into immediate communication both with the Waterloo and Hungerford Bridges.*

The route required a long viaduct, and the cost of the project was estimated at £280,000, with a further £400,000 required for land purchases, the latter sum being shared between the SER and L&SWR. It was hoped the connection could be completed within three years. But unfortunately for the SER, their scheme was opposed by landowners, and the project failed to receive parliamentary backing.

THE CHARING CROSS RAILWAY COMPANY

The SER's strategy of avoiding the L&GR's exorbitant fees soon turned in their favour. Deprived of this lucrative income, the L&GR began to suffer increased financial strain. They succumbed in 1845 and made a deal to lease their lines to the SER, thus allowing the company to muscle in on London Bridge.

With this stepping stone achieved, the SER were now keener than ever to push their line westwards, and in 1856 an application to do so was submitted, under the heading 'London Bridge and West End

Bricklayer's Arms terminal, 1844.

Railway'. This proposal sought to convey the railway from London Bridge station to a point 'at, or near a vacant piece of ground adjoining the Waterloo Road station of the London and South Western Railway Company, and near the junction of Vine Street with the York Road…'.

The following year, a report by the chairmen of the Eastern Counties Railway Company entitled 'Suggestions for Improving the Railway Communication of the Metropolis' deduced it would be advantageous to construct a line crossing the Thames at Blackfriars, with branches on the southern side diverging west towards Waterloo and east to London Bridge.

These two concepts were consolidated in February 1859 with the creation of the 'Charing Cross Railway Company' (CCRC), the formation of which was sanctioned by the SER. The CCRC's prospectus neatly summarized the plan, describing a route still familiar today:

> *The route… will extend from a junction with the South-Eastern at London Bridge, to a terminal station on the north bank of the Thames, near Charing Cross, and also to a junction with the South-Western Railway at Waterloo station.*

This project, estimated at £800,000, was approved in the summer of 1859. It involved one particular condition: that a physical connection be created between the lines of the L&SWR and the SER.

Hungerford Bridge and Market

The construction of a terminal at Charing Cross signalled the end for Hungerford Market, a trading site that had existed since the 1680s. The market was named after the Hungerford family home, which had stood on the spot until it was destroyed by fire in 1669. According to Samuel Pepys, the blaze was caused 'by carelessness of the girl sent to take off a candle from a bunch of candles, which she did by burning it off, and left the rest, as is supposed, on fire.'

The remains of this house were taken over by a market, which expanded with the creation of a piazza. This in turn was replaced

Hungerford Market, 1850.

by a newer building in the early nineteenth century, which was damaged by a further fire in 1851. This, coupled with the fact that the market was already in decline, meant there were few qualms in sacrificing the site for the railway. Those traders affected were given three months' notice, and were graciously permitted to 'take with them on their removal all trade or shop fixtures which they may wish to carry away.'

The site was also known for the original Hungerford suspension footbridge across the Thames. Designed by Isambard Kingdom Brunel, the bridge opened in 1845; however, its existence was short-lived as the arrival of the railway necessitated its removal in 1859. However, the cables from the bridge can still be seen today – in Bristol, where they were reused on the Clifton suspension bridge.

By the early 1860s construction of the line from London Bridge to Charing Cross was underway, and in 1861 powers were secured to obtain a further extension to Cannon Street. With this sanctioned, it appeared that the L&SWR's long-held ambition of having Waterloo directly connected to the City was finally coming to fruition.

THE CONCOURSE TRACK

In August 1861, at the CCRC's half-yearly meeting, the following announcement was made:

We have lately arranged to commence the works near the Waterloo station, with the object of connecting our railway with the South-Western system, from which we naturally anticipate considerable advantages, and there is every reason to believe that the connexion, when formed, will prove of very great convenience to the public.

This physical connection, a railway junction linking the SER and the L&SWR, was made above John Street and William Street (since renamed Alaska Street and Sandell Street).

To complete the link, the track was carried on an iron bridge (still visible today above The Welling-ton pub), through an archway and then – most unusually – directly across Waterloo's pedestrian concourse.

The concourse track was connected to Waterloo's central platforms, the ends of which contained gates that could be swung shut when the SER junction was not in use (which, as it transpired, was most of the time).

Although tenuous, this set of rails meant it was now technically possible to conduct a direct journey between Southampton and Dover. The junction was in place by 1863 (before Charing Cross officially opened), and was used on occasion by VIPs and royalty.

After being inspected and deemed safe by Captain Tyler, the link was used in this manner for the first time that year by the Crown Prince and Princess of Prussia for a journey between Windsor (where they had been visiting Queen Victoria) and Dover. This unique trip was reported in the press:

The Royal train will leave Windsor this morning by the South-Western Railway at 6.30am and pass through the Waterloo Station at 7.10. It will then proceed along the Charing-Cross Railway, pass London Bridge Station at 7.18, and thence by the South Eastern Railway to Dover.

Alaska Street.

Bridges over Waterloo Road: the red bridge carried the line between Waterloo Junction and Waterloo's main concourse, the blue bridge carries the South Eastern line, and the grey bridge is a modern pedestrian walkway connecting the two stations.

The track that ran directly across Waterloo's concourse can be seen in the foreground of this nineteenth-century photograph.

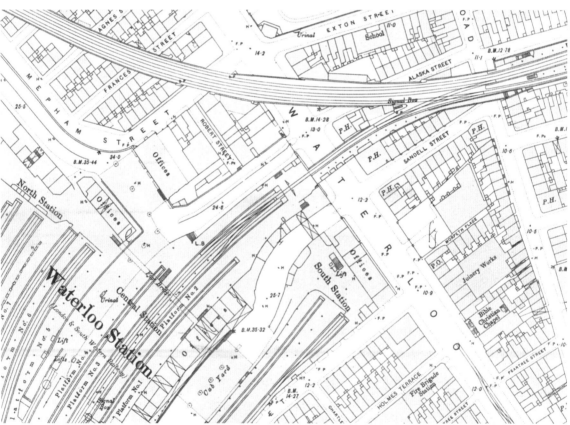

The track across Waterloo's concourse is detailed in this 1890s map; it can be seen running from platforms 2 and 3, and bridging Waterloo Road.

Compared to the route usually taken by Her Majesty's guests on their journeys between Windsor and Dover, it is stated that there will be a saving of more than an hour between the two points...By the new route the journey will be performed in 2 3/4 hours, without shunting.

On rare occasions, the line across Waterloo's concourse was also used by military traffic. Thanks to this purpose, the unusual connection warranted a mention in H.G. Wells' 1898 masterpiece, *The War of the Worlds*, in which a troop train, en route to confront the Martians, rumbles across the concourse:

About five o'clock the gathering crowd in the station [Waterloo] was immensely excited by the opening of the line of communication, which is almost invariably closed, between the South-Eastern and South-Western stations, and the passage of carriage trucks bearing huge guns and carriages crammed with soldiers. These were the guns that were brought up from Woolwich and Chatham to cover Kingston.

There was an exchange of pleasantries: 'You'll get eaten!' 'We're the beast tamers!' and so forth. A little while after that a squad of police came into the station and began to clear the public off the platforms...

THE EUSTON LINK

Although it was a rare sight to witness trains slowly chug along Waterloo's concourse, there was a brief period when a regular service did occur. This was thanks to the complex West London Extension Railway (WLER), which opened in March 1863.

The origins of the WLER dated to the 1840s, when the West London Railway was built between Harlesden and Kensington. Although little used at first, powers were granted to extend the line in 1859; this was a joint enterprise between the London & North Western Railway, the London, Brighton & South Coast Railway, the GWR, and the L&SWR, and it looked to bridge the Thames at Battersea in order to link the railways of the north and south.

Waterloo was connected to this line in July 1865. This allowed a circuitous service to be enacted, which ran from Euston around to Waterloo, and then, via the line across Waterloo's concourse, to London Bridge. This new route was described in an August 1865 edition of the *London City Press*:

In the early part of the past month a service of trains between Euston and London-bridge via Kensington and Waterloo was commenced, together with an arrangement of local trains between Waterloo and London-bridge.

Another report in the *London Evening Standard* indicated that ten trains per day operated on the route between Kensington, Waterloo and London Bridge, and fourteen between Waterloo, Blackfriars and London Bridge. The SER, however, were reluctant to accommodate this arrangement, and it was soon diverted to Cannon Street. Despite this – and no doubt due to the inconvenience of having regular passenger trains running across a pedestrian concourse – this circular route was discontinued on 31 December 1867.

BLACKFRIARS ROAD

Charing Cross station – situated approximately half a mile north-west of Waterloo – was officially opened on 11 January 1864. However, although the London Bridge to Charing Cross line swept past Waterloo, and the L&SWR and SER were now physically linked by a junction, there was little effort from either company to capitalize on their proximity, and it would be some time before the station now known as Waterloo East would come into being.

With this lack of co-operation, and the creation of an actual station at Waterloo Junction still some years off, passengers had no means of transferring between the two lines. Despite this, the CCRC had a stop-gap in development: the original Blackfriars station (sometimes known as Blackfriars Road station). A precursor to Waterloo East, Blackfriars was an elevated station on the southern side of the Thames (not to be confused with its later northern counterpart). An early mention describing its location appeared in the autumn of 1860: 'The Blackfriars station will be on the north side of Rowland Hill's chapel, and the road will be crossed by a flat girder bridge.'

Rowland Hill's chapel was a famous circular church (a shape supposedly chosen so the devil would have nowhere to hide) situated on the junction of Blackfriars Road and Union Street, opposite present-day Southwark tube station. It was later turned into a famous boxing venue named 'The Ring', managed in the early twentieth century by Bella Burge – aka 'Bella of Blackfriars' – who is believed to have been the world's first female boxing promoter.

Sadly, The Ring was destroying during the Blitz: bomb damage from that fateful night can still be seen pitted across the façade of the former Blackfriars station. The site of The Ring is now occupied by Transport for London's Palestra building.

By late 1863 construction of the line between Charing Cross station and London Bridge was complete, and an examination 'of the most rigid character' was conducted by government inspector Captain Tyler on 30 December. A number of interested parties went along for the ride, including a journalist from the *London Evening Standard*, who gave a brief description of Blackfriars station, saying it had 'two side and one central platforms lighted by globular lamps similar to those on the Metropolitan Railway'.

The station was also described as 'handsome and commodious', and as the 'great intermediate station of the line' where a great deal of traffic was expected.

Former Blackfriars station.

Things seemed rushed, however, and although the bricklayers and carpenters had finished their work, the painters had yet to start.

Blackfriars station officially opened in January 1864. At the same time, ownership of the CCRC passed to the SER – although the bold 'Charing Cross Railway' signage remained, and can still be seen outside the disused station today.

Approximately ten minutes' walk from Waterloo, Blackfriars station offered a useful if not somewhat disjointed link for those wishing to transfer between the L&SWR and the SER. However, it would prove to be very short-lived, and it closed after just five years when Waterloo Junction opened in 1869.

WATERLOO JUNCTION STATION

In February 1868, just a few weeks after the short-lived Euston loop had closed, it was agreed in an L&SWR board meeting that:

> ...*a proper passenger station ought to be placed at the junction of the branch with the Charing Cross main line; that the South Eastern Company's trains should stop at such station, and set down and take up passengers to and from this company's railways, as well as local passengers, at fares properly in accordance with those charged by the South Eastern Company between Charing Cross and their other stations.*

The L&SWR were clearly becoming agitated that the connection – which would provide them with their coveted link to the financial Square Mile – was gathering dust.

The SER, however, were reluctant to oblige, leading the L&SWR to force their hand by reminding them of their obligations under the Charing Cross Act, which had called for passengers wishing to transfer between the two lines to be accommodated. The L&SWR placed further pressure on the SER by introducing a bill that looked 'to invest the South Eastern with the necessary powers for providing station accommodation at the Waterloo Junction.'

As a compromise, the SER finally agreed to build a station on their line opposite Waterloo, as described in a bill that was read before a committee on 27 March 1868:

The South Eastern will erect a station at Waterloo and efficiently work it, and will charge the Charing Cross fares for the time being, and will commence the work as soon as may be. They will provide the means of passing between the Waterloo station and the new station.

Construction of Waterloo Junction, under the SER's chief engineer, Mr Ashcroft, was swift (perhaps indicative of the company considering it a hassle, and eager to 'get it done') and was almost complete by the end of the year. The speed of the project was evoked in a December edition of *The Builder* magazine:

Few public works are ever conducted in the sight of many thousands of daily spectators, or make such rapid and palpable progress, as has been the case of those which have been for a few months past in course of progress near the Waterloo junction of the Charing Cross Railway.
    The daily traffic has continued uninterrupted during the construction of three of the longest platforms, partly covered, connected with any railway station in or near the metropolis, exclusive of the terminal stations.

The article also noted that the 'new station has no architectural pretensions', and the viaduct upon which it was constructed ran 'through house property of a mean character and over narrow back and side streets'.

Waterloo Junction opened with little fanfare on 1 January 1869. Its layout was similar to the former Blackfriars Road station, which it replaced. The booking office, waiting rooms and other facilities were all located at street level, and accessed via Waterloo Road. The platforms above were basic, described as having 'earthen floors', which, 'open as they necessarily are all round, will, in winter or severe weather, be cold and comfortless for those who may have to wait for trains.'

1880s map showing Waterloo, Waterloo Junction and the surrounding routes.

This point seemed proven one month later on 3 February, when a writer using the pseudonym 'One Who Uses the Line Daily' wrote to the *London Evening Standard* to complain of the lack of shelter. Although praising the new station for its convenience, this correspondent also claimed it was:

About the worst you can find when you have to wait five or ten minutes for a train… The south side had been left entirely unprotected from the wind and weather, so that the luckless traveller who has to wait for a train on a wet or windy day has anything but a pleasant time of it.

The original junction that linked to Waterloo's concourse remained in place and was accessible from the southern end of Waterloo Junction's down platform. However, as reported, there was no change in the frequency of its use, in that 'this junction will not be used for ordinary passenger traffic, but for the Royal family, for troop trains, through goods, horse boxes, invalids, and other special purposes.'

Napoleon III Meets Waterloo

One dignitary who passed through Waterloo Junction was Emperor Napoleon III, who used the VIP connection in March 1871 en route to a meeting with Queen Victoria. One can only wonder what went through his mind as the train on which he sat slowly rolled along the concourse of a terminal bearing the name of a battle in which his uncle had been trounced.

Napoleon III died in Chiselhurst in 1873, and fifteen years later, in January 1888, his body – along with that of his son, who had died in 1879 – were removed in order to be reinterred in a new tomb at Farnborough.

For this, an elaborate funeral train was used, which paused at Waterloo Junction whilst it was handed over to the L&SWR for transfer via the concourse line. As the train entered Waterloo, a number of French gentlemen were standing by to salute the coffins and lay wreaths.

All the platforms at Waterloo Junction were 18ft wide and 3ft above the rails, bringing them almost in line with the floors of the carriages. Each platform was partially sheltered, with a 200ft long, flat roof, covered in zinc and supported by cast-iron columns. They were also decorated with a 'vandyked frieze'.

The platforms were connected by a subway, approached by an incline on the station's far western

Waterloo East, platform D.

Waterloo East connecting walkway.

end. This subway, described in a contemporary account as a 'dismal place', gained an unsavoury reputation and was replaced with overhead access in 1897.

As well as the entrance at street level, Waterloo Junction was, like today, connected to the main Waterloo station by 'a continuous covered way', which ran along the bridge between the two stations. A booking office for those using this route was located at the end of the walkway, on the southernmost platform.

At first, trains ran between Charing Cross and Cannon Street every ten minutes. The new interchange was a success, and in February 1869, *The Daily Telegraph and Courier* employed an interesting metaphor to describe the success of the newfound co-operation between the two companies:

> *The South Eastern lion and the South Western lamb may be seen at any hour of the day lying down together at Waterloo Junction, and growing fat on the unwonted combination of good temper and good sense.*

An Embezzlement Scandal

In the late summer of 1899 police raided Waterloo Junction to arrest five ticket collectors: Albert Warrington, Henry Simon, George Coulter, William Thomas Rowland and Russell Munday. The group were accused of embezzling money received as excess fares. Warrington, for example, was accused of receiving 18s 6d in one day, having only accounted for 3d.

Naturally the SER took the matter seriously, as the ruse had been systematic and prolonged. Warrington, who had taken the lion's share of the ill-gotten gains, pleaded guilty at Southwark police court and received six weeks' hard labour.

The rest of the group also pleaded guilty. The barrister representing Munday explained that his client had worked for the company for twenty years, yet only earned 23s a week and that 'the low wages had tempted him'. Coulter used the same defence, claiming that out of the same sum, he had to pay 9s a week rent. All men were sentenced to twenty-one days' imprisonment.

REDEVELOPMENT OF WATERLOO JUNCTION

Despite its financial success, Waterloo Junction station remained grubby and windswept for many years. Its condition was subjected to a rather scathing attack in a September 1880 edition of the *Pall Mall Gazette*:

> Their [the SER] junction station on the Charing Cross line with the South Western at Waterloo – a station which brings in a very large revenue to the South Eastern – is exposed and miserable to a degree hardly credible for those not familiar with it.
>
> A very few pounds would suffice to remove many of these discomforts, and would moreover afford space for advertisement placards, the rents of which would repay the outlay several times over.
>
> But the South Eastern are as obstinately blind to their own interest, as they are obstinately deaf to the complaints of a crowd of their best customers; so men, women, and children are left to the mercy of the wind and weather day by day and hour by hour...

The poor facilities at Waterloo Junction mirrored those experienced by travellers at its larger neighbour some forty years before, and it was soon clear that Waterloo Junction would also require widening

and new station buildings, powers for which were sought in the late 1890s.

The redevelopment was also spurred on by the opening of the Waterloo & City Railway (*see* Chapter 6), unveiled in 1898, and which offered passengers a warmer, drier and overall more modern onward journey. This competition meant that Waterloo Junction had to buck up its ideas.

The remodelled station came into being around the turn of the twentieth century, doubling its accommodation. A new booking office appeared on Sandell Street (the same street-level entrance that exists today), as did a cloakroom, luggage transfer office and hydraulic lift.

Waterloo East Sandell Street entrance.

The connection between Waterloo and Waterloo Junction was widened with a covered bridge, inclined to allow for easier transfer of luggage. A new platform was also added, along with glazed roofing to combat the elements.

The under-used connecting track running across Waterloo's concourse was finally severed in December 1911. This event seemed to concern *The London Daily News*, who pointed out that the link 'had distinct strategic importance as one of the means by which in a time of national emergency troops could be drafted on to the lines leading to Dover.'

In July 1914, just weeks before the outbreak of World War I, its removal was still lamented by some, as demonstrated by R. Langton Cole, who wrote to *The Globe* saying, 'If the South of England should ever be overrun by a foreign foe, that little bit of railway might be badly missed...'.

INCIDENTS AT WATERLOO JUNCTION

For most of its life, Waterloo Junction/Waterloo East has enjoyed a good safety record. One early notable incident involved that of a station master, forty-year-old Francis Young, who, on the evening of 13 December 1881, in heavy fog, was struck by a train and killed whilst attempting to check if the signalmen were at their posts.

Francis, who lived close by on York Road, left a widow and four children. Following his death, a fund was quickly started, which raised an impressive £760 for the family – over £93,000 in today's money.

The deadliest accident at Waterloo Junction occurred in the autumn of 1913. At around 8.50am on Saturday 25 October, the 7.25am service from Blackheath to Charing Cross was standing on the up platform. Due to dense fog, the train had been delayed and was awaiting the signal to proceed to Charing Cross. As it waited, the 7.32 service from Elmers End ploughed into the back of the stationary carriages. A contemporary report from *The Times* provides a vivid account of the crash:

The noise of the impact was heard in Waterloo station of the South Western Railway and in Waterloo Road. There were the mingled sounds of grinding brakes, breaking glass and splintering timber, followed by the cries of onlookers and frightened and injured passengers.

At the end of the stationary train were a third-class and a second-class coach, which, it is stated, were put on behind the guard's van in order to deal with the heavy traffic.

The third-class carriage was lifted up by the force of the collision and driven into the second-class coach, so that the roof of the latter was tilted up at an angle on top of the third-class coach, the flooring of which fell out. Some of the seats were forced through the roof of the carriages, and part of the over-hanging portion of the station roof and the end of the platform was carried away.

As luck would have it, a detachment of the St John Ambulance Brigade, who were due to attend Sandown races, happened to be at Waterloo at the time and rushed to the scene, where they turned Waterloo Junction's refreshment room into a makeshift hospital. Three people were killed in the collision and another twenty-four injured, two seriously.

FATAL RAILWAY ACCIDENT AT WATERLOO JUNCTION.

The breakdown gang at work clearing away the debris at Waterloo Junction after the smash, in which three were killed and nineteen injured.

Aftermath of the Waterloo Junction accident, 1913.

In November, an inquest into the collision was held at Lambeth Coroner's Court, where the jury determined that the deaths were due to the negligence of a signalman named Moore, although his actions were not felonious.

A less severe incident occurred in October 1926, when a service from Charing Cross derailed just outside Waterloo Junction. Although no one was hurt, the mishap left carriages teetering perilously close to the edge of the viaduct over Frances Street (a lost thoroughfare that once stood opposite St John's Church), leaving local residents fearing they might tip off the edge and smash into their homes.

TWENTIETH-CENTURY SCHEMES

As we can see today, the layout and purpose of the station that today's passengers know as Waterloo East has changed little since its original inception. An interesting point of note is that the platforms are not numbered: instead they are denoted by the letters A, B, C and D so as to avoid confusion with their much larger neighbour.

There have been several schemes mooted over the years that, had they come to fruition, would have changed the station beyond recognition – or indeed, seen it demolished altogether. The Charing Cross Bridge scheme, for example, was introduced in the 1920s, and envisioned a new road crossing spanning the Thames on the site of the old Hungerford Bridge.

Had this gone ahead, it was planned that Charing Cross station would be demolished and moved to a new location beside Waterloo, the large site completely consuming that occupied by Waterloo Junction. The plan received serious backing, and a bill was put forwards by the London County Council (LCC) in order to push ahead. This was rejected by a Commons Select Committee, however, and, not helped by the unfolding Great Depression, the plan quietly faded away.

A similar proposal was put forward in 1986 by architect Richard Rogers (designer of the Pompidou Centre in Paris and Lloyd's Insurance HQ in London). This, too, suggested demolishing Hungerford Bridge and Charing Cross station and relocating it to the area occupied by Waterloo East. A new footbridge would have been built, beneath which it was hoped would be a 'shuttle transport system' for the purpose of whisking people between Trafalgar Square, the Strand and Waterloo.

One aspect of this scheme – the pedestrianization of Trafalgar Square's north side – did eventually come to fruition, although thankfully Hungerford railway bridge remained untouched.

British Rail Class 411 in 'Jaffa Cake' livery at Waterloo East, September 1986.

CHAPTER 6

Waterloo Underground

In 1898 Waterloo became the first London terminal to be directly connected to a deep-level 'tube' line. This was the Waterloo & City Railway (W&CR), a shuttle service between the terminus and Bank Junction, which finally solved the L&SWR's ambition to have a smooth, direct link with the financial Square Mile. Today, of course, we know this as the Waterloo & City line, the shortest on the London Underground network.

However, the W&CR was by no means the first attempt at building such a railway from Waterloo.

THE WATERLOO & WHITEHALL RAILWAY

The world's first subterranean railway opened in London in 1863. This was the Metropolitan Railway, which initially ran between Paddington and Farringdon. This pioneering enterprise was constructed using the 'cut and cover' method, in which the tunnels were broad and relatively shallow. Services were hauled by steam locomotives, which meant that regular ventilation shafts had to be incorporated.

The Waterloo & City line,
Waterloo station.

In January 1865, two years after the Metropolitan Railway opened, *The Times* reported on a new underground project that was under consideration: the Waterloo & Whitehall Railway (W&WR), a short shuttle service linking the terminus with the heart of British government. The plan was groundbreaking, for it envisioned a tunnel far deeper than those achieved by cut and cover. As steam could not be used at such depths, the railway was to be a pneumatic one (electricity as a means of propulsion still being some years off). This report is from *The Times*, dated 12 January 1865:

The tunnel admits a full-sized omnibus carriage, which is impelled by a pressure of the atmosphere behind the vehicle, produced by lessening the density of the air in front.

It is an underground railway worked without locomotives. The proposed line will run in a tunnel under the Thames, and open a communication between Whitehall and the Waterloo station, near Vine Street. As a means of communication between one part of London and another this line will be quite an experiment.

Pneumatic propulsion had already been witnessed in London: a 2ft gauge Post Office despatch tube between the City and Euston had opened in early 1863, whilst a short experimental tunnel, capable of conveying passengers, had been demonstrated between August and October 1864 in Crystal Palace Park. The W&WR therefore seemed a natural progression of this technology.

Work Begins

A prospectus for the W&WR was published in June 1865, in which it was announced the railway 'will cross the bed of the river in a watertight iron tube'. This tube was to be constructed by Messrs Samuda, with other work on the line conducted by Messrs Brassey and Co. Optimistically it was estimated the works would be completed within one year. Once the line was open, it was hoped the carriages – which were to be 'commodious and well lighted' – would run at three- to four-minute intervals.

Pneumatic Tube Travel

The pneumatic railway at Crystal Palace was open to those brave enough to experience a journey through a 600-yard (550m) long tunnel. A detailed account of this novelty appeared in *The London Illustrated News*, describing the single carriage as long and comfortable, like 'an elongated omnibus capable of accommodating some thirty or thirty-five passengers'.

Entrances to the carriage were at each end and accessed via glass doors. Around the rear of the carriage was a metal framework, attached to which were bristles to aid the escape of air; one can imagine how these bristles would have sounded as they brushed against the tunnel.

The Crystal Palace pneumatic railway, 1864.

Air pressure was controlled by a set of iron gates 'which fly open' as the carriage approached. The 600-yard journey lasted approximately fifty seconds, although faster speeds were said to be possible. The report also noted 'it is supposing that the motion is much steadier and pleasanter than ordinary railway travelling…'.

Construction of the W&WR pneumatic tube on the Isle of Dogs, 1860s.

Thames opposite College Wharf (occupied today by the northern end of Jubilee Gardens), the river was dredged so as to make way for the foundations of a pier into which the tube tunnel was to be laid.

Over at Scotland Yard meanwhile, the area planned for the location of the north terminus was enclosed in preparation for building work.

Towards the end of the year it was reported in *The Morning Advertiser* that groups of piles had been driven into the Thames bed, denoting the sites for the piers and the route of the line. These were located a short distance from Charing Cross Bridge, both on the north and south side of the river. The same article provided further details:

The estimated cost for the project was £135,000 – approximately £18 million in today's money – far cheaper than the sums involved for the Metropolitan Railway. Newspaper reports from the time lauded the scheme, although the *Dundee Courier* did opine that the public 'might hesitate to patronise a gigantic blow-pipe of many miles in length'.

After receiving parliamentary assent, construction commenced on 25 October 1865. At a point in the

Running from the station in Scotland Yard, the line will be carried in brickwork beneath the tunnel of the Metropolitan District Railway, and then under the Low Level Sewer to the northern abutment.

From this, iron tubes of 16ft. diameter are to be laid on the clay beneath the river. The trough in the bed of the river is now being dredged for

View across the Thames from College Wharf (now Jubilee Gardens).

Fig. 6.—Section of the Pneumatic Passenger Railway under the Thames River, London.

(1.) Subway for Gas and Water Pipes. (2.) Sewer. (3.) Metropolitan Underground Steam Railway. (4.) Pneumatic Passenger Railway, now in course of construction. The Pneumatic Railway extends from Charing Cross, and passes under the Thames River to the Waterloo Road Station of the Southwestern Railway. The engraving represents that portion under the Thames embankment which has been finished.

Contemporary artist's impression of the W&WR.

the tubes. From the south abutment the line will be completed to the Waterloo station in brick-work, passing on its way beneath the Belvedere and York roads to a terminus near the South-Western Railway station.

At the cab entrance to Waterloo station on the York Road will be the pumping station, where the engines &c. are to be erected for work-ing the traffic.

Again, the report stated that the line would be ready within twelve months – and even hinted it could be extended towards Newington Butts.

FINANCIAL CRISIS

Despite initial optimism, work on the W&WR began to deteriorate rapidly, largely thanks to the financial crisis caused by the collapse of the Overend, Gurney & Co. Bank. On 20 January 1866 it was estimated that the time of completion was now likely to be many months off, and 'great dissatisfaction' had

been expressed at the progress made. In November the company applied for an extension of the time of completion, and also sought authorization to increase capital.

Further headaches occurred when the project was brought into conflict with the Metropolitan Board of Works, who, under the guidance of Joseph Bazalgette, were busy on the north bank of the Thames laying London's desperately needed sewer network – the path of which obstructed the W&WR. With Bazalgette's sewers requiring re-routing, it was determined that the W&WR should pay 'to do the works affecting the completion of the Northern Thames Embankment forthwith, or the board would do it for them, and charge them with the cost.'

In a board meeting held on 14 December 1866, it was announced that work on the W&WR was now at a complete standstill due to a lack of capital – and 'some strong remarks' were applied to the engineers. So desperate had the situation become that it was suggested that, as the tunnel was already partially laid, it should be turned into a toll-operated pedestrian footway so that shareholders' investments would not be lost entirely.

The following year the W&WR went cap in hand to the L&SWR: after all, the line was due to be of great benefit to them. The sum they sought was £33,000 – but their appeals came to nothing.

By 1869 the piles that had been driven into the Thames still remained in place, yet were now derelict and considered a nuisance. Despite work grinding to a halt, the company had been granted an extension until July 1870, meaning these obstructions could not be removed until then. Nevertheless, at a board meeting held on 8 July 1869 it was decided to dissolve the W&WR, which meant that the 'unsightly stack of wooden piles which stretch across the Thames' could finally be demolished.

Aftermath

In a final dig at the company, one journalist writing the following month quipped: 'If the Whitehall and Waterloo Company mean business, the best thing they can do is to pull their sticks out of the river bed and sell them for firewood.' The project, although bold, had failed.

In the early 1870s, an auction was held on York Road outside Waterloo where items from the scrapped scheme – including 'pile-driving engines and monkeys...a centrifugal pump...warehouse cranes...scrap iron...timber...an anvil...skips...nuts and bolts...and navvy barrows' – were sold off.

In the early 1960s, remains of the W&WR were discovered close to Waterloo when construction on the Shell Tower commenced.

THE CHARING CROSS AND WATERLOO ELECTRIC RAILWAY COMPANY

In the early 1880s the idea of connecting Waterloo and Whitehall via an underground line was revived, this time by a new company: the Charing Cross and Waterloo Electric Railway (CC&WER). Their proposed route was almost identical to the one attempted by their predecessor, the only difference being that it would have run slightly further, passing

Sir Wilhelm Siemens.

beneath Northumberland Avenue and terminating at a point close to the statue of King Charles I, just south of Trafalgar Square.

The plan was notable in that it intended to power the trains using electricity: had the project been successful, it would have been the first railway in London to have done so. The idea was in good hands, as it was supported by the electrical engineer Sir Wilhelm Siemens, brother of Werner von Siemens who had pioneered electric railways in Germany.

The CC&WER generated considerable interest. In an article dated 6 April 1883 the *Pall Mall Gazette* championed the idea of using this new method of power:

The advantages of electricity as a motor in tunnels are too obvious to need explanation. At one stroke all the sulphurous fumes and the stifling steam which render the underground railway so horrible are avoided. There is no shrieking, no puffing and groaning, no dirt, no damp; everything is clean and dry.

The same article also provided details as to how the line would be built: the tunnels would be 'composed of iron caissons lined with white bricks, and lighted, it is to be hoped, with incandescent lamps.'

Powers to construct the line were granted, and permission was also sought to extend the line eastwards towards Blackfriars and the City – the route now followed by the present-day Waterloo & City line.

Sadly, Sir Wilhelm Siemens died in November 1883, and the loss of his tutelage deflated interest for the project; by 1885 the scheme was shelved.

FINAL OVERGROUND ATTEMPTS

Ten years before the W&CR was proposed, there had been a final push to directly connect Waterloo to the City via an overground line. This attempt consisted of two schemes that were practically identical, yet pursued by different backers. Both were presented as bills to parliament in November 1881.

The first proposal was the for 'Waterloo & City Railway' (not to be confused with its later subterranean namesake), which looked to extend the South Western line towards a terminal on the southern side of Great St Thomas Apostle Street, 'about 33 yards westward from the junction of that with Queen Street' – in other words, a stone's throw from Cannon Street Station. It was suggested the line could be carried on a viaduct through Lambeth and Southwark, before spanning the Thames on a three-arched crossing close to Southwark Bridge.

The second proposal was the 'South Western & City Junction Railway' (SW&CJR), which, had it been approved, would have been built either by the L&SWR or a new company specially formed for the purpose. The SW&CJR looked to follow the same route as its competitor, the only difference being it was anticipated the extension would merge with tracks belonging to the Chatham and Dover line.

Both proposals faced considerable opposition due to the disruption they threatened. *The London Evening Standard*, for example, whilst noting the advantages of extending beyond Waterloo, warned that should such a project be given the go-ahead, it would result in 'the demolition of an enormous amount of property in the district', and that it would be 'difficult to see what would be left of some of the parochial territories in Southwark and Lambeth'.

The two schemes were examined by a parliamentary committee in December 1881, where it was concluded that the interests of those in the affected parishes should be considered as of paramount importance.

Meanwhile, a petition opposing the railway's extension was drawn up by St Saviour's Board of Works, who held a meeting to discuss the matter at a hall on Emerson Street in early 1882. They needn't have worried, however, as both bills were withdrawn shortly after this opposition was organized.

The determining factor in scrapping the two schemes was down to cost: the SW&CJR, for example, estimated the price at £2,800,000 – approximately £331,000,000 in today's money. To put this into perspective, *The Times* pointed out that the extension would be less than 3 miles (5km) long, yet in rural Northumberland it was possible to construct a line that was 78 miles (125km) in length for a mere £1,240,000.

A final overground proposal was pushed in late 1891: the Waterloo & Royal Exchange Railway (W&RER). Interestingly, this was put forward at the same time as the underground scheme was being promoted, and was therefore seen as a competitor. The route of this line would have run past The Cut, Nelson Square and along Union Street before turning north, crossing Southwark Street and stopping to serve a local station beside the Hop Exchange. It would then have continued across the Thames (between London Bridge and Cannon Street Station), and terminated at a point in the south-western corner of Bank Junction.

The W&RER believed that, by being above ground, their railway would be a far more pleasant alternative to tube travel. To make their scheme more attractive, they also promised to incorporate a pedestrian walk-way on their Thames crossing to alleviate congestion on London Bridge. However, at an estimated £3,600,000 this was also deemed too costly, and the plan was abandoned in early 1892.

THE WATERLOO & CITY RAILWAY

London would have to wait several more years for a successful deep-level tube: this arrived in 1890 with the opening of the City & South London Railway (C&SLR). Forerunner to the present-day Northern line, the C&SLR ran between Stockwell and the now defunct King William Street. Construction was achieved thanks to the 'Greathead Shield' – named after its inventor, South African born James Henry Greathead – which enabled tunnelling at far greater depths.

When the C&SLR opened, the directors of the L&SWR would have paid close attention: here was a modern, efficient service capable of whisking commuters directly into London's Square Mile, a link which had long eluded Waterloo. The C&SLR thus paved the way for the Waterloo & City Railway (W&CR), and a bill seeking powers to build 'an underground electrical railway one mile four furlongs 680 chains in length' was presented to parliament in December 1891.

The estimated capital required was £540,000, and there were initial rumours that the line would be cable-hauled, something that Greathead himself admitted had potential.

Opposition

The only real opposition to the W&CR emanated from the SER, who were unhappy that the proposed route was similar to that already established between Waterloo Junction and Cannon Street (*see* Chapter 5).

In May 1892, the SER Board branded the W&CR 'inconsistent with good faith', especially as the L&SWR had 'received immense benefit' from

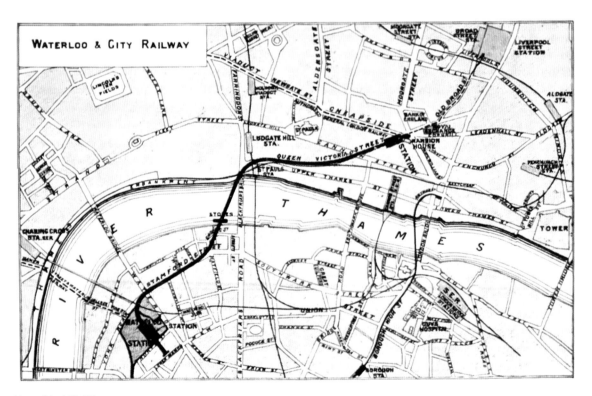

Map of the W&CR's route.

Waterloo Junction 'without contributing one penny either to the cost of the railway or of the Cannon Street station'. In the face of progress however, the SER's bitterness counted for little, and their opposition was tempered somewhat in March 1893 when, at a select committee in the House of Commons, it was stated that 'it was not intended to place any stations on the route of the line, but merely to have terminal stations at Waterloo and the Mansion House.'

The W&CR also had the backing of the mighty Corporation of the City of London. By the summer of 1893 royal assent had been granted and construction could begin, although work would not commence until 18 June 1894.

BUILDING THE WATERLOO & CITY RAILWAY

The contract for forging the new subterranean line (sometimes referred to in the press as the 'South Western extension into the City') was awarded to John Mowlem & Co. Ltd, who by this point had carried out work on Billingsgate Market, Smithfield Market, the Woolwich Ferry and Liverpool Street Station. The contract amounted to £222,064 and stipulated that the work was to be completed within thirty months.

James Greathead, creator of the revolutionary tunnelling shield, was brought on board, as was veteran L&SWR engineer William Galbraith. To dig the tunnel, borings were required at four points along Stamford Street, along with the corners of Waterloo Bridge Road, Cornwall Road, Princes Street and Duke Street. Meanwhile, 18,000 tonnes of foundry work for the line were ordered from Stockton-on-Tees.

The project provoked the curiosity of many Londoners, who sought the few signs above ground indicating the line's progress, the most popular vantage point being Blackfriars Bridge. Here, spectators could see the piles that had been driven into the Thames, along with a large works platform positioned in the middle of the river.

View from Blackfriars Bridge.

On 19 November 1894 a humorous encounter describing a youngster considering the 'iron sheds and the structure on which they are placed in the bed of the Thames' appeared in the press: '"Them there sheds," the urchin said, hanging over Blackfriars Bridge and pointing up the river, "why, them's goin' to be a cirkiss – a 'lectric cirkiss."'

The same article goes on to describe how, beneath the calm of the river, 'deep below, the undisturbed surface of the Thames, in the very bowels of the earth, the calm and the monotony of the surface are not to be found.'

Indeed, deep below in the stifling heat, navvies were slowly pushing through the clay with Greathead's hydraulic shield, lining the tunnel behind

Airlock used during the construction of the W&CR.

them with cast-iron rings. Four shields were in use. Having been placed in the middle of the route, two pushed tunnels towards Mansion House, whilst the other pair churned their way towards Waterloo.

The work was carried out twenty-four hours a day, 'except between six o' clock on Saturday evening and midnight on Sunday.' Lighting was provided by electricity, and for a time, a system of compressed air – which required workers to pass through an airlock – was utilized in order to reduce the risk of subsidence.

The excavated material was placed in wagons and hauled by a fleet of small electric locomotives towards the works platform near Blackfriars Bridge. Upon arrival at the bottom of the shaft, the little trains would blast a signal, prompting the wagons to be hooked on to chains and hoisted out via a steam crane. The waste would be tipped on to a barge and carried away to be dumped on Dagenham marshes. The Blackfriars platform also allowed materials to be delivered by river.

By June 1895 the two tunnels were advancing at a rate of 100ft (305m) per week, although by February the following year this figure had slowed to 73ft (22m).

In January 1896, the works were paid a royal visit by Belgium's King Leopold, who donned overalls before being given an hour-long tour through 'the dark and solemn depths'. Leopold was said to be highly satisfied with what he saw, leading him to contemplate a similar system for Antwerp.

Sadly, on 21 October 1896, James Greathead died before he could see the project completed. He was fifty-two years old. Today, a statue of him can be seen on Cornhill, close to Bank Junction where his pioneering work centred. Below ground at Bank, in the subway linking the Docklands Light Railway to the Waterloo & City line, it is also possible to view part of the tunnelling shield used in construction of the W&CR, which was unearthed in 1987.

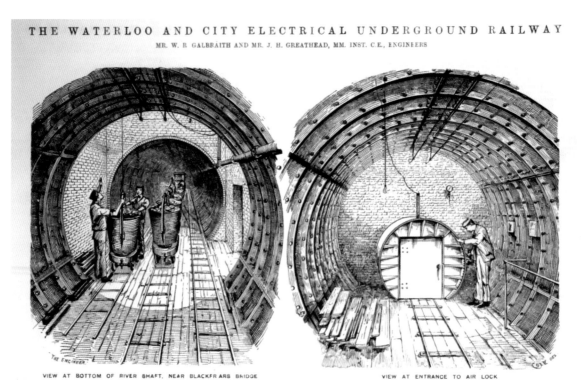

THE WATERLOO AND CITY ELECTRICAL UNDERGROUND RAILWAY

MR. W. R GALBRAITH AND MR. J. H. GREATHEAD, MM. INST. C.E, ENGINEERS

VIEW AT BOTTOM OF RIVER SHAFT, NEAR BLACKFRIARS BRIDGE

VIEW AT ENTRANCE TO AIR LOCK

Construction wagons, and a view of the airlock when closed.

James Greathead statue; the plinth acts as a ventilation shaft for Bank station.

EARLY ROLLING STOCK

Whilst workers toiled away deep beneath London, moves were made above ground to acquire the rolling stock that would serve the line. This was a matter that generated considerable controversy, as the carriages were ordered from an American firm: the Jackson & Sharp Company of Wilmington, Delaware.

According to the W&CR, seven English firms were invited to tender. However, 'not one of them was able to complete and deliver the rolling stock of only 22 coaches in the time fixed for the opening of the railway' (although there was some consolation in the fact that the wheels and axles were to be supplied by English and Scottish firms). This revelation led to calls in Parliament that any company granted consent to build a new railway should be required to purchase 'a fair proportion of the goods required in the United Kingdom'. The caveat was refused.

In October 1897, *The Gloucester Citizen* reported that the W&CR carriages were nearing completion, and that the Jackson & Sharp Company had also been awarded a number of contracts with other English firms – including a saloon car for the SER. This led them to lament:

> *Whilst we see the spectacle of industries paralysed through a lock-out, on one hand, on the other hand we see a large branch of industry go to America, for which wages might be earned here.*

The American-built carriages were fashioned mainly from wood. Seven could be coupled together, providing seating capacity for 350 people. The motors were located at the end of the car, over which seating was built. These end seats were positioned facing each other, whilst those in the rest of the car were set in rows.

In order to reach the end seats, passengers had to mount a small set of steps, meaning you could sit either 'upstairs' or 'downstairs'. The seats were also

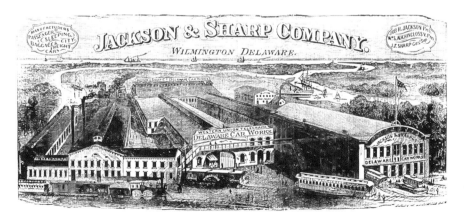

Jackson & Sharp Company, USA.

75S W&CR works locomotive.

THE LINE OPENS

Ten days after this tragic accident, the W&CR was officially opened by the Duke of Cambridge, on Monday 11 July 1898: this date happened to mark the fiftieth anniversary of the opening of Waterloo station itself. The Duke arrived at Waterloo at 1pm, and was 'conducted down the slightly inclined passage near

wooden – 'for the sake of cleanliness' – and were described in one account as resembling the 'third-class dining cars which run on the long journeys on the northerly lines'. These carriages remained in service until 1940.

A separate electric locomotive – the 75S – was also ordered by the W&CR. This loco, made in Woolwich by Siemens Brothers and Co, operated at night to deliver coal to the line's power station at Waterloo, and also to shunt passenger stock. It remained in use until October 1968, when it suffered electrical burnout; it is now held by the National Railway Museum's Shildon branch.

A Fatal Accident

By summer 1898 construction was complete and the finishing touches were being added. Empty trains were also being run back and forth in an experimental capacity. Unfortunately, on 1 July this resulted in a fatal accident.

Two workmen, Frederick Farmer and James Moody, were in the Waterloo depot, busily drilling holes into one of the carriages for the purpose of installing an electric motor. As they worked, a test service entered and was directed into the wrong siding, where it rammed into a stationary carriage, sending it crashing forward into the car upon which Farmer and Moody were working. Both men were pinned between the cars. Farmer died instantly, whilst Moody's thigh was crushed, although after receiving treatment in St Thomas's Hospital, it was reported he was able to return home by cab.

Providing Power

On the line's opening day, *The London Evening Standard* provided a detailed account of the power station then used to generate electricity for the line:

> *The Power station is well located in Launcelot Street, externally to the eastern side of the London and South Western Terminus in a sufficiently open and accessible place. It is divided into generating house, boiler house, and depot.*
>
> *The first, a solid and internally white glazed brick building about 12 feet long, and of proportionate width and height, is formed by a cross road-way into which two portions of pit-like appearance.*
>
> *In the further portion are six sets of Belliss steam engines coupled direct to Siemen's continuous current dynamos. Each dynamo yields a current of 450 amperes at a pressure of 500 volts. The cables which conduct the current to the trains are hung in festoons, one above the other, on the inner face of the southern wall, and are controlled by a fine switch board beside the generating plant.*

This power plant became obsolete in 1915 when the L&SWR electrified their mainline routes; when this occurred, power was drawn from a new plant based on Durnsford Road. However, the old power station was maintained on standby in case of emergencies.

No. 9 platform to the departure platform of the new railway.'

The W&CR's station was described as spacious, lined with white glazed bricks and ample illuminations. The Duke and his party of guests then made the journey to the City, which was described as 'exceedingly pleasant' – in those early days, the tunnels were painted white and illuminated along their entire length. On arrival the company 'ascended the steps and had a momentary peep at the busy world above'.

The return journey was then made, and 300 people sat down to lunch; this included 'wines of the choicest description' in the W&CR's large Waterloo booking hall, which was bedecked in flags and banners for the occasion.

The Duke by this time was almost eighty years old, and after a toast to Queen Victoria, he rose to make a speech in which he declared he'd been present when King William IV had opened London Bridge sixty-seven years previously in 1831. He continued by saying that he was glad he had lived long enough to 'accompany the chairman and those who were assembled that day in traversing a tunnel railway connecting the Waterloo terminus with the City of London.'

The Duke joked that if, sixty years ago, 'anybody had ventured to predict that London was likely to see such a railway, he would have been considered a fit subject for a lunatic asylum!' He then concluded with a toast, proposing 'Success to the Waterloo and City Railway!'

Despite this royal blessing, the *St James's Gazette* was quick to criticize the new line. Just one day after the ceremony, they bemoaned the fact that, unless an individual had business in the City, 'it is of very little use', and 'we do not understand why a station was not made at Blackfriars'.

Although officially opened, there was some delay in having the line ready for public use due to a labour dispute in Wales, which hampered delivery of the carriages. The line finally opened at 8am on Monday 8 August 1898.

Fares cost 2d single and 3d return, with services running from Monday to Saturday, from 8am to 10pm. Interest was high, with thousands of people flocking to see the new line; so large were the crowds that policemen had to be stationed at each end to direct the traffic.

The London Evening Standard praised the W&CR, declaring it to be already a huge improvement on the C&SLR, which had opened just a few years before. The light inside the carriages was bright enough to read in comfort, and they also noted that a number of improvements were already in the pipeline, including 'increased smoking accommodation'.

W&CR, 1898.

Waterloo & City line entrance hall.

At Waterloo, there were initially five entrances to the W&CR, all of which converged on the booking hall. One was accessed via Waterloo South's cab yard, a second from the Central station's cab yard, a third at the northern end of Waterloo, and two further entrances outside via York Road and Aubin Street, a now lost road once situated on the terminal's southern side.

On the evening of the line's opening, the station superintendent at Cannon Street (which provided the older, overground connection to Waterloo Junction) was asked if the new line had yet impacted bookings on the SER. He declined to provide such information, although another official insisted (one can imagine somewhat irritably) that 'their trains did the journey in a shorter time than that taken by the new line.' By February 1899 there had already been 1,555,000 recorded journeys on the W&CR.

The only slight mishap occurred on 10 October, two months after the line opened, when a train halted in the tunnel, causing some panic amongst passengers, who claimed they were experiencing suffocation. Although the stoppage occurred close to the City station, this led one person to write to *The London Evening Standard* to ask 'what means there are for the supply of air', should a stoppage occur in the middle of the tunnel.

In 1903 the system experienced a notable dip in passenger numbers. This was attributed to the Paris Metro fire disaster, which broke out close to Couronnes station on 10 August of that year, claiming eighty-four lives. Naturally this disaster made many at the time question the safety of what was then a still relatively new form of transport.

INTO THE TWENTIETH CENTURY

After the opening of the Central London Railway (now the Central line) in 1900, a pedestrian interchange was soon made with the W&CR at Bank. Back at Waterloo meanwhile, an escalator linking the mainline platforms to the W&CR was installed in 1919.

In 1922, the controversy over the cars' American design finally received some respite when the

Electric Tramway Company of Preston were contracted by the LSWR to build four extra trailers. As noted in *Railway Magazine*, the British designs were rather different to the earlier US versions.

In 1940 the W&CR's old wooden cars were finally retired, and after years of serving below ground, were taken outdoors to be stored at two sites, one at Eardley Sidings close to Streatham Common, and the other near Gatwick. At least two of the cars remained rotting in this manner at Eardley Sidings until the late 1940s. All were eventually broken up, and none of the original stock survives.

In the late 1930s the route underwent a modernization programme. This involved replacing the old semaphore signals with lights, improving driver communication (via an emergency 'pinch wire'), and, most notably, ordering new rolling stock. The new carriages were built at the Dick Kerr Works in Preston, and constructed from steel. They came into service on 27 October 1940, and were of larger capacity and with wider doors to facilitate quicker boarding and alighting times during rush hour.

At the time, the line was operated by what was now Southern Rail, meaning they were painted in the company's dark green livery. Years later, after nationalization, they received a new coat of paint, this time British Rail blue. The cars were unique as their ends were not painted in 'warning yellow', the reason being that, because they operated completely underground, such a feature was deemed pointless.

A further colour scheme appeared in the late 1980s, this time the bright blue Network South East coat.

Waterloo & City line Class 487 at Bank, 1984.

Interior of Class 487.

Class 487 in British Rail and Network South East liveries, Eastleigh Depot, 1986.

In and Out

The Waterloo & City line is the only London Underground line to operate completely below ground, the depot at Waterloo itself being subterranean. Therefore on the rare occasions that rolling stock requires removal from the system, heavy lifting gear is required. At first this was achieved with a lift, provided by W. Armstrong & Co. of Newcastle (who had also provided luggage lifts elsewhere in Waterloo station). Situated at the end of sidings on Waterloo's northern perimeter, the lifting gear was water-powered and capable of lifting 30 tonnes. In the early 1990s, this lift vanished beneath the site of the Eurostar terminal.

Armstrong lift, 1984.

Today, carriages are hauled out via a crane, which is located on Waterloo's southern side, on Spur Road, close to the junction with Baylis Road.

Another interesting feature of the Waterloo & City line is the Travolator at Bank station. This was opened on 27 September 1960, and was Britain's first moving walkway. Prior to that, access to the line had been via a long, sloping tunnel, the bane of many a City gent. For those wishing to experience this steep climb, the original walkway still exists parallel to the Travolator. A similar moving walkway was installed at Waterloo following the extension of the Jubilee line.

Waterloo & City line crane.

The Travolator at Bank station.

The original passage at Bank, which now runs parallel to the Travolator.

The 1940 cars, which were eventually designated British Rail Class 487, remained in service until 1993, after which they were replaced with 1992 tube stock. One of the 1940 units is preserved at the London Transport Museum's Acton depot.

Due to being operated by the L&SWR/Southern Rail and then British Rail, and with its unique rolling stock, the Waterloo & City line – which came to be nicknamed 'The Drain' – was something of an anomaly when compared to the rest of the London Underground. On many tube maps, the line was not included in the key, having instead *Waterloo & City Railway* (or later, line) written on the map itself, alongside the British Rail logo. The line was finally taken over by London Underground in 1994, after which it adopted the turquoise colour scheme.

Class 487 at London Transport Museum depot, Acton.

WATERLOO'S OTHER TUBE CONNECTIONS

Waterloo is connected to three other tube lines: the Bakerloo, Northern and Jubilee, each of which would require their own separate books in order to cover their full histories. Here, though, is a brief overview of their Waterloo stories.

The Bakerloo Line

The history of the Bakerloo is closely tied to Waterloo, the line's name being an amalgamation of its original, official title: 'The Baker Street & Waterloo Railway' (BS&WR).

As with the W&CR, planning for the BS&WR commenced in the early 1890s, and at a parliamentary committee held on 1 June 1892, engineer James Henry Greathead spoke in favour of the scheme. There were, however, objections from the Metropolitan Railway and also that arch nemesis of the L&SWR, the SER.

At the select committee, a Mr Littler QC rubbished the idea of such a line, stating that 'the proposed railway merely constituted an omnibus service, which could not possibly be made to pay'. But any opposition was soon overcome, and permission to proceed with construction was granted in March 1893 with The Baker Street & Waterloo Railway Act.

As we can see today, a portion of the Bakerloo line – namely in the vicinity of Charing Cross and the

Embankment – closely follows the route of the abandoned CC&WR and partially constructed W&WR. In fact there was initially some early opposition to the BS&WR from the National Liberal Club, whose building stands close to where the W&WR was initially intended to terminate.

As with the W&CR, there was some controversy over the fact that the BS&WR's first cars were built in the USA – in this case by the American Car Foundry Company (although the parts were assembled in Manchester). *The Nottingham Evening Post* was particularly scathing of the American design, comparing their appearance to 'a converted goods wagon' and describing the design as 'both a commercial and unpatriotic blunder'.

Shortly before the line's opening, the cars were drawn by horses (with each carriage requiring a team of fourteen) through London to the depot near St George's Circus, just south of Waterloo.

The line was opened by the then Chairman of the LCC, Sir Edwin Cornwall, on 10 March 1906, and originally served stations between Baker Street and Lambeth North (then known as Kennington Road), one stop south of Waterloo.

The name 'Bakerloo' caught on before the line had even opened. Perhaps the earliest mention comes from an edition of *The Globe* newspaper, dated Tuesday 6 March 1906, which contained a tongue-in-cheek column entitled 'By the Way', in which, amongst other quirky takes on news, a line simply said: 'Suggested name for the new tube – The Bakerloo Railway.'

When it first began serving Waterloo, access to the Bakerloo was via a lift, with the main entrance being located on York Road.

The Northern Line

The Northern line reached Waterloo in the 1920s when the then C&SLR and Charing Cross, Euston and Hampstead Railway agreed to forge a new connection by building a branch between Euston and Kennington. This opened on 14 September 1926, creating what was then the world's longest underground railway tunnel.

At the time of writing the Northern line is currently being extended towards Battersea; in autumn 2021 a station is due to be opened at Nine Elms, a short distance from the original, pre-Waterloo L&SWR's terminus.

Nine Elms Northern line station under construction, 2020.

The Jubilee Line

The Jubilee line is the most recent addition to Waterloo. Tunnelling reached the station in September 1995, and the service opened to the public four years later. This was, of course, part of the Jubilee line extension that had been mooted for many years but did not receive the go-ahead until the early 1990s.

An interesting feature of Waterloo's Jubilee line ticket hall is the wire-mesh sculpture of an elephant, positioned above the escalators. This was created by Kendra Haste at the turn of the twenty-first century, and was originally displayed at Gloucester Road Station. The elephant's re-siting at Waterloo is thought to be a nod to Astley's Amphitheatre, an

Kendra Haste's elephant sculpture.

early circus ring once based in the area (on the eastern end of Westminster Bridge Road) between 1773 and 1893.

CHAPTER 7

Transformation and World War I

With the W&CR providing a direct underground link with the City, the L&SWR finally seemed content to accept Waterloo – which by the 1890s employed 600 workers – as a terminal. However, as detailed in Chapter 3, the haphazard way in which Waterloo had grown throughout the nineteenth century meant that the station was a bewildering muddle. As well as inconveniencing passengers, the station's complex layout hampered the smooth running of services, resulting in frequent delays.

To address this, further powers for widening the lines into Waterloo were applied for. As for the building itself, drastic change was needed if Waterloo were to be the L&SWR's flagship. And so began what was dubbed the 'Great Transformation', an immense scheme of remodelling and reconstruction that would eventually transform the station into the Waterloo we recognize today.

Waterloo, 1900.

INITIAL PLANS

In 1897, the initial plans to expand Waterloo – towards Lower Marsh and Waterloo Road – were rejected, curiously because they did not go far enough. Although unopposed by the LCC and approved by the House of Lords – who believed the work would bring about public improvements – the L&SWR soon baulked at their scheme owing to the huge sum required in order to purchase the necessary land and property. They therefore revised the project, asking for powers to develop within a more confined area.

At a select committee held on 17 March 1897, this scaled-back plan was rejected after being branded 'ill considered', and far too altered from the one that had already passed through parliament. The L&SWR were advised to apply 'mature deliberation' and come back in the next session with a bill 'more worthy of the object sought to be obtained'.

Deliberate they did, and in January 1898 it was announced that:

> ...the South-Western will, in the coming session of Parliament, seek for powers to acquire extensive areas of property in Lambeth, so as to further greatly enlarge Waterloo station.

OPPOSITION

In February 1898 it was announced that property was to be acquired around Lower Marsh, Westminster Bridge Road, Cornwall Road, Morpeth Place, Newnham Terrace, Aubin Street, Granby Place and Griffin Street. Using these areas as a rough footprint, the size of the new Waterloo – along with the widening of its approaches – was clearly going to be immense, causing immediate alarm amongst local residents who, under threat of being displaced, hastily arranged a petition.

Their concerns were supported at a parliamentary committee, where a Mr Willis insisted that, should permission be granted for work to proceed, it was imperative that 'nothing short of a definite undertaking to re-house the people who will be displaced by the pulling down of houses' should be implemented.

Granby Place.

Mr Willis then went on to say that he was himself a resident of North Lambeth, and could 'tell the Vestry that the district had suffered from the depredations of this company [the L&SWR] for many years.'

This opinion was rebuffed by a Mr Turner, who reassured the committee that the L&SWR 'was not composed of a set of rogues'.

The following month, a meeting was held at the Lambeth Vestry Hall, Kennington Green (the precursor to Brixton Town Hall), a report of which dramatically referred to the 'Railway Moloch at Waterloo' – Moloch being a term associated with child sacrifice. At this meeting it was pointed out that in the course of previous expansions, the L&SWR had already destroyed 1,500 houses and done nothing to replace them.

It was suggested therefore that pressure be placed upon the Home Secretary to 'refuse his consent to the removal of the old buildings until the company had provided other dwellings for the people who had been displaced.'

The Vestry's opposition was successful: in July 1898 a select committee decided the L&SWR's case for the enlargement of Waterloo station was not proven. Consequently, requests to purchase property in the space bounded by Belvedere Road, Westminster Bridge Road and Waterloo Road were struck out of the bill.

The L&SWR vowed to approach parliament again in the following session, to which Lambeth Vestry responded they would continue to oppose such plans – unless the provision was made that new dwellings be erected before the old ones were demolished.

In early 1899 the bill was once again put forward. In reference to this submittal, it was noted at an L&SWR board meeting that:

...the accommodation at Waterloo, both for the public and their officers, was very limited, and they hoped Parliament would see its way to give them the powers they sought, which would enable them to make adequate accommodation in the interests of all concerned.

The plans – which would create the biggest station in the country – proposed to evict about 2,000 working-class people, which once again drew the ire of Lambeth Vestry.

There were, however, supporters of the enlargement. The *St James's Gazette*, for example, in an article dated 10 February 1899, declared that the L&SWR's continued push for expansion was something to be thankful for. Reminding readers as to why it was necessary, they described Waterloo as being more complex than Clapham Junction, and that 'a long and careful training is required to master its intricacies…'.

The Gallant Colonel

The campaign against Waterloo's expansion was spearheaded by Lieutenant Colonel Ford, who represented North Lambeth for the LCC. In an interview with *The South London Press* dated 4 March 1899, the Lieutenant was quoted as saying that those residing in the vicinity of Waterloo were under threat from 'being hunted out of their homes like rabbits from a warren', and he made it clear that he was determined 'to defend the poor and artisan classes' who faced not a single penny of compensation.

Colonel Ford was adamant that residents should be entitled to remain at Waterloo, for 'these poor people must live near where their daily bread is earned – I refer, as instances, to the employees at Covent Garden markets and the Strand theatres.' He went on:

They [the L&SWR] want to run amuck of the district! Listen to this. Roughly speaking, the company ask Parliament to let them take for their private purposes and for dividend making the following: The property of the north side of the railway between Westminster Bridge Road and Griffin Street; the property between Griffin Street and York Street; the property from the west of York Street to within 50 yards of York Road; the property between Addington Street and Westminster Bridge Road.

The company also propose (it really beats anything I ever heard of) to take away from the public (without compensation to the Lambeth Vestry) the whole, or portions of the sites of the

Launcelot Street.

following public streets and highways: Griffin Street, Little York Street, Aubin Street, Holmes Terrace, Christies Place, Chartley Place (you see, they are going for the poorest homes – those least able to raise even a feeble protest), Launcelot Street, and Granby Place! These streets represent an area of 10,600 square yards, and in a district, too, where homes for the workers are most needed.

In summary, Colonel Ford believed the L&SWR were laying 'violent hands on areas, not necessarily the most convenient, but the cheapest to acquire, because they were occupied by the poor.'

He was also convinced that the company would soon be forced to abandon their scheme.

CLEARANCE BEGINS

Despite concerns over the number of homes requiring demolition, the expansion of Waterloo was inevitable. In May 1899, at Vestry Hall, Kennington, Lambeth Vestry announced they had been liaising with the L&SWR's solicitor, Mr Bircham; the result of this meeting was that an agreement had been reached that new dwellings should be in place before any families were evicted.

The following month, the L&SWR's bill for enlargement was presented to the House of Lords, the details of which included:

The effect of the enlargement will be to increase the area covered by the terminus from fifteen and a half acres to twenty-three acres; to provide four additional platforms, making fifteen in all; to increase the length of platform facing lines from 3,523 yards to 5,737 yards, and afford seven additional passenger lines, which, with the seventeen already existing, will number twenty-four in all. A new road of 60 feet in width will also be constructed for vehicular traffic entering and leaving the terminus.

The cost of these works was estimated to be £700,000 – over £90 million in today's money. To help their cause, the L&SWR also said they were prepared to pay £30,000 to the LCC for the purpose of improving areas affected by the works.

One of the first buildings earmarked for demolition was All Saints Church, which stood on Leake Street, close to the junction with Lower Marsh. Despite being only forty years old the church – which could seat 2,000 people and was claimed to have the finest sculpted marble reredos in all of south London – was described as being 'exceedingly dilapidated'.

It ceased to be an ecclesiastical building on 31 October 1899 (although it was not demolished until 1901), and the parish was absorbed by St John's Church, Waterloo Road. The original Necropolis station (*see* Chapter 4) was also torn down.

By the end of August 1900, a site for the new housing had been chosen: a 4.5-acre (1.8ha) site on Westminster Bridge Road, occupied by the engineering workshops of Maudslay, Sons and Field, who specialized in manufacturing marine steam engines. The flats, designed for 1,200 people, would be named 'Campbell Buildings'. New blocks were also erected on Boniface Street (for 290 people) and Miles Street (for 800 people).

Two schools, which replaced ones lost to the remodelling of Waterloo, were built to serve the new amalgamated parish of St Anne's and St John's. One of these was located in Archbishop's Park. Whilst a new building was being prepared, pupils from a school formerly based on Hercules Road were, for a time, taught within a number of Waterloo's railway arches. According to the headmaster, Mr Wood, this understandably proved somewhat problematic, although his pupils 'appreciated the situation immensely'.

In October 1902 the Home Secretary detailed what he regarded to be reasonable rents for these new properties. However, his decision attracted great controversy; as the *Daily News* reported:

Members of both parties [in a meeting at Lambeth Borough Council] joined in roundly condemning him for what he regards as reasonable rents to be paid by poor tenants. Half a guinea for three rooms and seven-and-three for two rooms to be paid by people who barely earn

WATERLOO *CIRCA* 1900

At the turn of the twentieth century, the area around Waterloo was still seen as impoverished and, in some cases, dangerous. In February 1900, the *Cardiff Times* gave a detailed account of the vicinity:

Is this London? Oh, what a dingy, grimy place! Is it not wonderful people should say that when they leave Waterloo station, the huge terminus of the South-Western Railway and find themselves in one of the long dismal streets which lie thickly between the station and the gay, delightful, bustling, exciting London of our fancy.

The main thoroughfares are full of hurrying people and crowded with busses and cabs and carts; but nobody wants to linger on the way or to glue their faces to the windows of such shops they find...

Of the other streets, some are squalid, some merely dull and sordid; not one is in any way attractive and nobody lives or walks in them by choice. Some are lined with costers' barrows and the Saturday night market there is a thing to see and hear, only it is not advisable for well dressed strangers to loiter in the mob. It is a large parish, the vicar having about 12,000 people to look after, and I don't suppose there is a rich person among them all.

Houses in the Waterloo Bridge Road, 1880s.

The account concluded by noting that 'many a little boy and girl without enough food and clothing' could often be found shivering around Waterloo.

thirty shillings a week were characterised with no uncertain emphasis as 'monstrous charges' and 'outrageous rents'.

At the same time, the L&SWR – who operated the properties – were accused of being Draconian: laundry was prohibited on a Sunday, gas was promptly shut off at 11pm, and the company also insisted they could conduct inspections at 'any reasonable hour of the day'. The L&SWR defended this regime by arguing that their work to improve Waterloo meant locals would benefit from improved railway travel, as well as the overall improvement to streets and other facilities in the neighbourhood.

THE UNION JACK CLUB

At around the same time that the remodelling of Waterloo station was being planned, so too was the creation of another institution in the area, the history of which is intrinsically linked to the station's history: the Union Jack Club, which, in its present form, still stands, towering over both Waterloo and Waterloo East.

By the turn of the twentieth century, Waterloo station had become the terminal most associated with the armed forces, accommodating the movement of thousands of troops and sailors, a role bolstered between 1899 and 1902 by the Second Boer War. Soldiers and sailors – often en route between places such as Aldershot, Winchester, Southampton, Portsmouth and Plymouth – were a common sight at

The Union Jack Club, viewed from Waterloo.

the station. As such, both a naval and military picket policed the station at weekends to keep an eye out for any bad behaviour.

The idea of a club to support the many such men passing through Waterloo was suggested by Miss Ethel McCaul, and began to gain impetus in January 1902. As the *Army and Navy Gazette* described:

> *The club would be undenominational, meals would be provided, beer allowed, but there would be no bar or canteen. A leading feature would be the sleeping accommodation for men on furlough or passing through; and the use of a safe or lockers for the deposit of valuables, kits, clothes &c., would be a great convenience.*

The scheme was given the go-ahead the following year – by which point it was estimated that at least 100,000 troops passed through Waterloo per annum – with a budget of £50,000. The plans included 400 bedrooms, a restaurant, smoking room, reading room and a billiard room, all of which would be available for 'any man belonging to the Imperial forces...his uniform will be his passport'.

It was hoped the club would protect such men 'against the terrible trials and temptation to which they were exposed while in London', or to put it more bluntly, Waterloo at the time went, in some quarters, by the rather unfriendly nickname, 'Whoreterloo'.

Money for the club was raised privately and quickly, and included the use of fund-raising concerts. The club's foundation stone was laid by the Prince of Wales on 21 July 1904. The Union Jack Club was officially opened by King Edward on 1 July 1907, for which ceremony the entire area, including Waterloo Station, was festooned in flags and banners. The original building was fronted in terracotta and contained 200 bedrooms costing 3d per night.

In 1913, a second Union Jack hostel opened close to Waterloo on Secker Street. This building was intended for the use of wives and children of servicemen, the main club being for men only, and it remained in this role until the 1970s. The building is now owned by Imperial College.

THE FIRST PHASE OF REMODELLING

At an L&SWR meeting held on 5 February 1905, it was announced that the area to the south of the terminus had been cleared, paving the way for the foundation of 'what was practically a new station'. At another gathering in August it was announced that the works were making good progress, platform lengthening and the widening of tracks between Waterloo and Clapham Junction being amongst the first issues tackled.

The task of re-ordering what *The South London Press* referred to as an 'enormous railway jumble' was placed in the hands of the L&SWR's chief engineer J.W. Jacomb Hood, and his assistant R.D. Hawes. For his research, Hood travelled to the United States to garner information on modern station designs. Sadly he would not live to see the project to its full completion; he died on 6 March 1914.

As with the station's original construction in the 1840s, the marshy terrain proved problematic, meaning that a lot of the new land acquired had to be 'plugged deep'. The contractor tasked with the reconstruction was Messrs. Perry & Co. Ltd, who were based at 56 Victoria Street.

The viaduct over Westminster Bridge Road required significant upgrading and was expanded to carry eleven tracks (before, it had supported eight). Meanwhile, work began on rebuilding Waterloo's southern side.

To allow trains to continue running, the South station remained in use whilst the framework for its replacement (sometimes referred to in the press as a new 'wing') was built around it. Although this minimized passenger disruption, one journalist complained in 1908 that 'for many weary months the air has been rent with hammerings'.

Alongside this work, a small but significant improvement occurred in April 1905 when the District Messenger Company opened an office on Platform 3, thus allowing the public to send telegrams.

In February 1906, *The Daily News* provided an update on the progress, reporting that the foundations close to Lower Marsh had to be laid to a depth of 20ft (6m). A parcel depot, located beneath what was to be the new station, was already in place and the framework for the station itself was almost complete. The

Waterloo Station, 1900 – the steps seen here were nicknamed 'The Bench'.

Photo. World's Graphic Press

CANINE CHARITY.

London Jack III, the dog collector at Waterloo Station for the
Railwaymen's Orphanage Fund.

*London Jack III, one in a line of Waterloo's resident charity dogs,
who in the nineteenth and early twentieth centuries roamed the
platforms collecting money.*

report also described how 'the roof will be of glass
and ironwork, a lofty construction specially designed
to avoid the danger of any unexpected collapse under
any conceivable circumstances.'

This final point was a reference to Charing Cross,
the roof of which had suffered a collapse in December 1905, killing six people. However, Waterloo's
roof would be 70ft (21m) high, double that of its
predecessor.

By March 1907, a subway had been completed
beneath the platforms, providing access to both York
Road and the Underground lines, whilst to the south
a vehicular roadway was also in place.

Although the work was relatively uneventful, there
was at least one death during construction – that of
twenty-four-year-old Alexander Davis of Battersea,
who plunged from a set of scaffolding. At the inquest,
the coroner noted 'there was no doubt that this was

dangerous work, but there appeared to be no means
of avoiding it.'

On 27 June 1908 one of the new platforms was
used for the first time by the royal train, when King
Edward VII and Queen Alexandra journeyed to Salis-
bury. The couple were reported to show:

*...a keen interest in the new extension of the
station, asking many questions concerning it,
and before they entered the royal train they
expressed their appreciation of the magnitude
of the work and of the importance of the extension to the travelling public.*

In early 1909 the new and improved station was
almost ready to begin serving the public. In January
of that year, the *Westminster Gazette* provided an
in-depth look at the work:

*The improvement embraces, amongst other
features, a new entrance on Westminster Bridge
Road. Hereabouts it is found that the brick
arches which formerly carried the railway
overhead have been removed, and steel gird-
ers, supported upon a central row of columns,
substituted, so as to give a clear driving way
and increased height. This short covered way,
which is lined with white glazed bricks, leads
to a wide approach to the station, which being
on the high level, is reached by an easy gradient. Two spur roads branch off here to the
Lower Marsh, where there is another spacious
entrance, which, with one from the Waterloo
Road, gives access on the street level, to a large
parcel depot. On this last-named road, too,
there is a handsome new front to the terminus.*

The same report mentioned the 'very handsome and
substantial looking' roof, and also the new buffers
that 'will resist a train weight of 400 tons running at
ten miles an hour, and thus will be of especial value
at Waterloo, where there exists a falling gradient as
the station is entered.'

The new south wing (today the oldest part of
Waterloo station) opened on Sunday 24 January 1909,

Train at Platform 1, 2019.

and further works on the remainder of the station commenced soon after.

THE SECOND PHASE

The second major change completed at Waterloo was the new vehicular approach and pedestrian pathway from Westminster Bridge Road, which opened, without ceremony, on Monday 18 December 1911. This replaced the old Griffin Street entrance and served passengers bound for boat trains and main-line express services. The road (still in use to today) was operated on a one-way system, with vehicles leaving via the Lower Marsh exit. The new road would eventually be extended around Waterloo's northern perimeter, forming the road we know today.

Upon opening, the *Westminster Gazette* praised the new entrance, saying it was bound to encourage shops and businesses to the area. They also gave an evocative description of the dismal building it replaced:

> *The station has long been a straggling irregular collection of platforms, almost cut off from the surrounding roads, to which it should give easy access. On the one hand, from York Road, was a steep slope over which horses slipped*

Waterloo approach road.

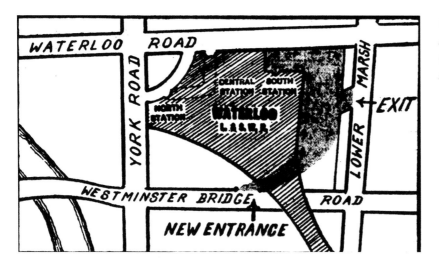

1911 map denoting Waterloo's new entrances – note that North, Central and South stations are still in place.

THE *TITANIC*

Due to its connection with Southampton, Waterloo played a small role in the *Titanic* disaster of April 1912. At 9.45am on Wednesday 10 April, a White Star Line boat train – a '*Titanic* Special' – departed Waterloo's platform 12 carrying well-to-do passengers bound for the doomed liner. Many of these passengers arrived at Waterloo from London's exclusive hotels; it was believed, for example, that between twenty and thirty parties had travelled from The Savoy alone.

Waterloo boat train (which connected to a liner bound for Canada) pictured in April 1912, days before the Titanic *disaster.*

According to *The Globe* (which they hinted, in hindsight, was a bad omen), this train was delayed: 'the engine, after drawing the train nearly out from the platform, suddenly stopped owning to a mechanical defect. It was some time before the locomotive could be restarted.'

Life on board *Titanic* was famously captured by Father Francis Browne, who documented his experience with many photographs. These included images taken at Waterloo of the awaiting train, and he also leant out of a moving carriage to snap a shot as the train finally got moving. Fate intervened for Father Browne when he disembarked in Ireland, shortly before *Titanic* headed out across the Atlantic.

Another *Titanic* link can be found with the famous image of Ned Parfett, the *Evening News* paperboy holding up the poster bearing the headline, '*Titanic* Disaster, Great Loss of Life'. Ned was born on Cornwall Road, just moments away from Waterloo station. Tragically he was killed in World War I less than two weeks before the Armistice.

and panted; from the Waterloo Road itself were narrow, dangerous alleys, steeper still.

The main entrance – speaking architectur-ally – was an entrance to nowhere in particular, leading only, by dark and dismal staircases, to a few suburban platforms. And an alternative route by which cabs could enter the station was through long and intricate tunnels, badly lighted, and, to everybody except the London cabman, seeming to call for exploration.

In the autumn of 1912, the designations of North, South and Central stations were finally abolished, meaning the platforms could be consolidated and their numbering streamlined from 1 to 18. From the following year, those wishing to bid friends and relatives farewell were required to pay for a one penny platform ticket, provided at the gates by newly installed vending machines.

In the summer of 1913 a collection of restaurants and tea rooms was opened within the station. *The Sporting Times* was most impressed with these new facilities, as this review from 3 July demonstrates:

For years we have known this spread-eagled station, but we hardly know it now, for it is rapidly being converted into an intelligible and

homogenous whole...Hitherto London, south of the Thames, has been practically devoid of restaurants of an appetising kind.

Today Waterloo provides a restaurant constructed and served on lines calculated to make the proprietors of the Piccadilly caravan-saries rub their eyes and say, 'Hallo! Now, how can we go one better?'

It is not for us to dwell upon the beautiful circular bar on the platform level, lofty though the theme might be. Rather let us ascend by lift to the realms above where the ladies' tea room and the elaborate luncheon and dining rooms are. These are large, airy, and handsome apart-ments, wherein you may find all kinds of provi-sions, hot and cold, and always of the most appe-tising description...The tradition of the railway refreshment room sandwich has been left behind, and here you will find catering on West End lines at – what shall we say? – well, suburban prices.

People coming from the South Western suburbs to the London theatres will now find at Waterloo excellent dinners and suppers available.

The main restaurant, featuring oak-panelled walls, neat white tablecloths and silverware, was open between 7am until midnight and charged 3s 6d for a five-course meal. A large selection of wines, spirits, liqueurs and cigars was also avail-able, and the venue quickly became a favourite with theatregoers.

Waterloo station restaurant advertisement, 1914.

THE EVE OF WAR

In July 1914 – just weeks before the outbreak of World War I – things were looking bright for Waterloo. The majority of the Great Transformation was complete, with the finishing touches being overseen by Alfred W. Szlumper, who had taken over following the death of J.W. Jacomb Hood in March 1914. The star attraction was the terminal's new roof, comprising 45,000sq ft (4,180sq m) of glass, provided by W.E. Rendle & Co. of Victoria Street.

Waterloo station concourse, 1914.

Other contractors, all based on Victoria Street, included Messrs Dorman, Long and Co., who had provided the steelwork, and Tredegars, who provided the electrical lighting, telephones and clocks. 'The all-important sanitary arrangements in the ladies 1st and 3rd class retiring rooms' meanwhile were created by George Jennings Ltd of Lambeth Palace Road.

As the project neared completion, the final cost came in at £2,000,000 – equating to approximately £232,510,204 today – a colossal amount for the time.

On 22 July 1914, *The Globe* wrote a glowing report on the new station. They concluded that 'The L and SW Railway':

> *...deserve the unqualified thanks of all travellers for the provision of a terminus that is in itself a thing of beauty and yet withal admirably adapted for the purpose for which it is primarily intended – a place of going and coming, whether on business or pleasure bent.*

But at the time this article was written, events on the Continent were rapidly descending into chaos. On 28 June, a young Serb named Gavrilo Princip had assassinated Archduke Franz Ferdinand of Austria in the city of Sarajevo, thus sparking a chain of events that would see the world plunged into World War I. For the next few years, many of those using Waterloo would

Selection of advertisements from contractors involved in constructing the new Waterloo, 1914.

Waterloo's platforms, 1914.

certainly not be bound for pleasure: they would be troops and sailors, headed for the horrors of history's first truly modern conflict.

WORLD WAR I

With the clouds of war gathering, Waterloo immediately found itself at the centre of the crisis. On 3 August, the day before Britain officially entered the war, thousands of civilians arrived at the station after a lucky escape from the Continent. *The Westminster Gazette* reported that:

> In Waterloo station the scene was…abruptly at variance with the customary Bank Holiday spectacle. No excursion trains were being run, and the station seemed to have been given over almost entirely to the movements of the military. Soldiers were in possession of several platforms, the gates either being shut or held by sentries.

The day after war was declared, posters appeared at stations on the L&SWR bearing an important announcement:

> The London and South Western Railway Company have to give notice that in consequence of the requirements in connection with the movement of His Majesty's Forces, it is not practicable to continue the whole of the Passenger Train Service as advertised…
>
> The Company also give notice that they are unable to guarantee the running or punctuality of trains, and cannot be responsible for any delay, loss or damage which may occur to passenger train traffic.

Early reports of troops being sent off to war were, as can be expected for the era, optimistic and bombastic. On 4 August, *The Daily Mirror* described the departure of sailors from Waterloo:

> The sailors, with curious-shaped bundles in their arms, smoked clay pipes and smiled good humouredly at the crowds, who would insist on cheering them. Husbands and wives and sweethearts exchanged embraces, while crowing babies, who appeared to be highly pleased at the general animation of the scene, were raised high in the arms of their fathers.

Nurses, too, gathered at the station in large numbers on their way to the Front. But by the end of the month the wounded were already being sent back – this, from the *Pall Mall Gazette* dated 31 August:

> Last night 117 men were taken from Waterloo station to the hospital where beds were awaiting them, and a further 300 arrived this morning. Their wounds are not of a serious character, being mostly in the legs and feet, but many of the men on arrival were suffering from exhaustion consequent upon their long journey.

Waterloo was a convenient centre for the wounded, as the huge King George military hospital, opened in May 1915, was located on nearby Stamford Street. Patients treated there wore a special blue uniform, and those well enough would often take a stroll to Waterloo to meet with fellow comrades.

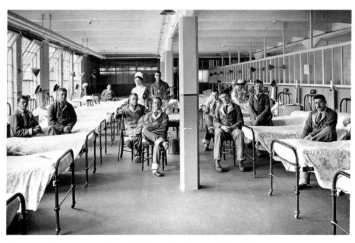

Ward at King George's Hospital, Stamford Street, World War I.

Waterloo also processed many horses en route to the battlefield. On one day alone in October 1914, 1,300 horses arrived at the station, along with wagons, which it soon transpired were unable to fit through Waterloo's entrance due to their tilts (coverings). This problem was solved by Captain the Earl of Carrick, who took to smashing off the obstructions with an axe. The horses were then loaded on to twenty-seven trains, which were dispatched over a period of twelve hours.

SHADOWED BY A NIGHTMARE...

Due to propaganda, reports of injured soldiers return-ing via Waterloo often glossed over the seriousness of the situation, and were often keen to emphasize that many were walking wounded. But on 25 September 1914, socialist magazine *The Clarion* published a slightly more realistic account of the terminal as it appeared in time of war, in an article written by Winifrid Blatchford:

On Wednesday Dorothea and I went to Water-loo station on the chance of 'something turning up'. Something did. Many a something.

We thought we might see some troops leaving for the front. Many had left the day before and we had missed them. We felt we would like to see them go, to wave them goodbye and provide them with some smokes.

We saw no troops leaving for the front. But we saw some recruits entrained for Aldershot, and many sailor men and some refugees and white-haired, red-faced khaki-clad soldiers saying goodbye to women and children, and some Cambridge University boys, hot and weary and caked with mud to the knees, returning from drill and rifle practices and long marches.

It was not Waterloo as we had known it since childhood. It was a Waterloo of dreams, shad-owed now and then by a nightmare. It was a sad and merry, alert and business like, comic and tragic Waterloo. Waterloo thronged with-out confusion or bustle, Waterloo very much

awake, very much in earnest, steeped in a strange atmosphere of quiet, determined, swift alertness. Waterloo with both eyes wide open and the expression of the face changing with every movement of the great finger on the great clock.

Another account comes courtesy of Robert Graves, who sustained such horrific injuries during the Battle of the Somme that he was initially believed dead. In his 1929 autobiography, *Goodbye to All That*, Graves describes – with a very cynical eye – his return to Waterloo as a wounded man:

I had wired my parents that I should be arriving at Waterloo station the next morning. The road-way from the hospital train to a row of wait-ing ambulances had been roped off; as each stretcher case was lifted from the train, a huge hysterical crowd surged up to the barrier... Flags were being waved. The Somme battle seemed to be regarded at home as the beginning of the end of the war.

Some years later, Dame Sybil Thorndike, who was due to perform at the Old Vic (which stands just across from Waterloo) one evening recounted an air-raid, and her desperation to get to the stage for fear of upsetting the formidable theatrical producer, Lillian Baylis:

Shall we ever forget the crashing night of the Air Raid on Waterloo Station? The Lear tempest raged that night... As I got out of the Waterloo tube station I met crowds pouring down the stairs with the Air Raid look on their faces, and in their talk too.

Lillian [Baylis] was more to be reckoned with, however, than any raid, so up I fought my way to the street. I was stopped by a bobby, who said: 'You can't go outside here, my dear; raid's on.' 'I can't help the raid' I cried, clinging to his brass buttons, 'the curtain's up at the Old Vic, and I shan't be on for my entrance.' 'Old Vic, is it' he said. 'Oh I know Miss Baylis; yes, you're right,' and a lull coming in the bomb sounds, he gave me a push into Waterloo Road with a: 'Now run for your life, and if you're killed, don't blame me – blame Her!'

ADAPTING TO WARTIME

As the months progressed, Waterloo settled into its role as a major cog in the war effort. As well as providing a key transportation role, a section of the arches deep beneath the station were converted into a stronghold for the safekeeping of government documents – an obvious choice considering Waterloo's proximity to Whitehall. This allocated space, which still exists today, was fitted out with strongdoors, whilst the corridors were built in a zig-zag fashion – similar to the pattern used in the trenches – as a means of hindering any potential invader.

Wartime storage stronghold beneath Waterloo.

In May 1915 the L&SWR began to employ female cleaners, and in December the same year, the London Society for Women's Suffrage established a canteen at the station where servicemen returning from

'The Hut'

The prefab hut that served troops at Waterloo later went on to be requisitioned as a place of worship in another part of the capital. This interesting project began in December 1922, when a Jewish gentleman named Mr Arthur Garman, upon moving to Keyes Road, Cricklewood, found it impossible to secure a seat at his local synagogue. Faced with a long waiting list, he decided to establish his own congregation.

Arthur and his supporters met at various temporary locations, including private homes. Before long it became clear that a permanent synagogue would be required, and a site was purchased on Walm Lane NW2 for the purpose. Whilst money was being raised to build the synagogue, it was decided to erect a temporary structure. As reported in *The West London Star*:

> *A subcommittee was appointed, and after numerous long journeys in and around London, a large war-time hut which stood at Waterloo station was purchased [for £1000], taken in parts and erected on this site where it stood for seven years.*

Not surprisingly, the temporary synagogue came to be nicknamed 'The Hut'. It remained in service until 1931, when the much grander Cricklewood synagogue was unveiled.

'The Hut' meanwhile was gifted to the Congregational Church on nearby Chichele Road, as the Reverend Kenward had come to the aid of the synagogue when it was being constructed. The church decided to move the hut to a site 'somewhere in the Wembley district'.

the Front could obtain a free meal. This buffet was supported by charity events such as special theatrical galas.

Around the same time, the City of London National Guard began a scheme in which forty of their members were placed on duty at Waterloo to assist troops with any queries – for example, how to deal with paperwork, exchange French money, and to generally play the role of Good Samaritans.

The Salvation Army also provided rest and free toilet facilities at Waterloo, which, by early 1916, had already been used by 20,000 servicemen. Outside the station, close to the Union Jack Club, the YMCA provided further shelter with a small hut, complete with canteen, which was open twenty-four hours per day.

On Waterloo Road, just a hundred yards from the terminal, a tattoo parlour run by a Mr Burchett did a roaring trade – including tattoos for women and, in some cases it would appear, children, as reported in a July 1917 edition of *The Graphic*:

> *One soldier, just before leaving for the front, brought his small daughter, aged nine, to Waterloo Road, and gave instructions for a shamrock and a thistle to be tattooed on each arm.*
>
> *'Without a flicker that child put her little arms on the table', says the tattoo-man, 'and never winced. Proud as Punch she was when it was all over, because "daddy wanted it done". Queer idea, but then I run up against lots of queer ideas in my tattoo shop.'*

Back at the station, the horror of war and its associated psychological trauma would occasionally stalk Waterloo's platforms, with a number of suicides occurring at the terminus. One such example was that of William George Mark Russell, who in October 1915 was found dead in a carriage at the station after shooting himself. At the inquest, George's brother-in-law, Joseph Parsons, stated that George 'was a man who had taken the war deeply to heart, and always looked on the black side of things. He seemed to be very depressed about the war.'

In December 1915, an extremely tragic incident occurred when Annie Louisa Ballard fell beneath a train whilst waving her son off to war. She was killed instantly.

Another shocking event occurred on 21 September 1918 when Milford Granger, an eighteen-year-old Canadian deserter, shot two police officers outside Waterloo after they attempted to arrest him for housebreaking. Fortunately their injuries were not fatal, and Granger was jailed for five years.

Due to the threat from Zeppelin airships (and, later in the war, faster Gotha bombers), a blackout was enforced in London. This meant that, by night, porters and passengers at Waterloo had to find their way around with dimly lit lamps. Despite this precaution, Waterloo did not altogether avoid being targeted by German bombs.

On the night of 29 September 1917 a raid succeeded in dropping two high-explosive devices on the station, one on the viaduct over Westminster Bridge Road, and the other on a siding alongside York Road. This resulted in considerable blast damage being done to the tracks and rolling stock.

THE ARMISTICE

After the guns fell silent on 11 November 1918, Waterloo still had its part to play. Shortly after the armistice, *The Ealing Gazette and West Middlesex Observer* reported an eye-witness account in which an Ealing resident 'heard the glad news while at Waterloo station'. This fellow noted that 'the only unhappy group there…was a party of recruits who had that morning joined up. But even they gave a cheer, deciding to make the best of it.' By the end of the war it was estimated that the L&SWR had handled 20 million troops.

On 26 November one of the first batches of returning prisoners of war – 500 men in all – steamed into Waterloo, where they were met by the Duchess of Bedford and gifted flowers, refreshments and cigarettes. The following month, the repatriation of Belgian refugees, who had been forced from their homelands at the start of the conflict, began at

Wartime Displays

In October 1915 a welcome respite from the station's war activities occurred when a vintage railway carriage was introduced to a plinth on Waterloo's concourse. The carriage, which dated from the 1830s, had served on the Bodmin & Wadebridge line (which was operated by the L&SWR) and was described thus:

Bodmin & Wadebridge carriage, which was displayed at Waterloo in the early twentieth century.

The under frames are painted a vivid red lined with black, while the coach body is dark blue, with yellow upper panels. The appearance of the vehicle is more like a stage coach in its elaborate colour scheme. The buffers are quite noticeable on account of their size, and are made of wood. The carriage is mounted on a length of original rail and stone sleepers.

This carriage remained in situ for some years and is now held by the National Railway Museum.

Also displayed at Waterloo, in May 1918, was an American army ambulance train, which the public could enter for the price of eightpence. 'Tasteful souvenirs descriptive of the train' were sold at the exhibit, the proceeds of which went to charity – including the L&SWR's orphanage.

Waterloo. One such refugee, interviewed by the *Daily Mirror*, stated: 'Our two countries will be friends for ever and ever now.'

It would understandably take some time to demobilize the vast number of troops.

Following the war, thousands of soldiers from the Indian Army found themselves encamped close to Hampton Court. On 16 August 1919, shortly before they were due to return home, these men were all taken by special trains to Waterloo and proceeded to march from the station to Buckingham Palace. Thousands of spectators lined the route, and at the Palace, the King addressed the soldiers, offering his gratitude for their service.

ELECTRIFICATION

Considering the stresses of war, it may come as some surprise to learn that it was during World War I that steps were made by the L&SWR to begin electrifying

4 Sub Unit (4732) on display at Waterloo, November 1986.

suburban routes into Waterloo. The idea had been considered before the war, and it was in 1916 that electric trains – on the Hounslow Loop – first appeared at the station. By 1922, electric routes were running from Waterloo to Barnes, Kew, Richmond, Wimbledon, Kingston, Hampton Court and Shepperton.

The lines used the third-rail system with a voltage of 600V DC. The electricity was generated by a special plant built at Durnsford Road, Wimbledon. The original rolling stock was all built for steam services, and converted for electrical use. At a board meeting held in March 1917, it was estimated that the conversion of steam to electric had achieved a saving of £75,000.

There was something of a hiccup, however, on 20 March 1919 when a steam train collided with an electric service just outside the station. Nobody appears to have been injured in this incident, which was blamed on the signalman, who claimed he allowed the electric train to leave the station and cross the path of the steam engine in the belief that it would 'have time to get out'.

Despite this modernization, steam locomotives for longer distances would continue to run from Waterloo until the 1960s.

COMPLETING THE GREAT TRANSFORMATION

Although much of the remodelling of Waterloo had been completed before the war, there were still some finishing touches required, and scaffolding and evidence of building work would remain at the station for several more years. A number of buildings were built between platforms 15 and 16, to be used as the stationmaster's office, staff rooms and for lost property. As they resembled small cottages, this area was dubbed 'the Village', a nickname that persisted with staff for many years after.

In July 1921, an article in *The Pall Mall Gazette* provided details of the further improvements appearing at Waterloo, including details about a new tea room – complete with an American soda fountain – that was decorated in a 'light and artistic style'. It was said that the kitchen serving this eatery 'would arouse fierce envy in the heart of any housewife', for it boasted a refrigerator, an unlimited supply of hot water, and 'the most perfect system of ventilation', which was described as 'delightfully cool' – all ultra-modern conveniences for the time.

A French Request

With what was essentially a new station nearing completion – along with the centenary of Napoleon's death, and the fact that France and Britain had secured a new friendship through war – in May 1921 the French newspaper, *Le Gaulois*, suggested that a name change for Waterloo was now in order:

> *The first thing which French people arriving via the Harve–Southampton route see in London is Waterloo station. This is the first word of welcome which London gives her French guests, and it is suggested that the present occasion might be taken to modify the name of the station.*

This suggestion was ignored by the authorities, although a response in *The Bystander* joked that the British public would still call the station Waterloo regardless. The same thorny issue would arise years later, with calls to change the station's name when Waterloo's international section serving Eurostar trains was introduced.

Charlie's Return

As Waterloo provided a key hub for those travelling between London and America, for several decades in the twentieth century the terminal became the 'go to' place for fans wishing to catch a glimpse of their favourite stars. With silent cinema booming in the early twentieth century, the biggest celebrity by far in the 1920s was Charlie Chaplin, who himself had been born not too far away from Waterloo, on East Street Market, Walworth, and had grown up close by in a small home on Methley Street, Kennington.

Charlie had moved to America in 1910 where his comedy shorts featuring the 'Little Tramp' quickly became a hit, providing much needed laughter during the dark days of World War I.

At 11.30am on Saturday 10 September 1921, Charlie returned for a visit to his home town where he was due to promote his masterpiece, *The Kid*, and was mobbed by a 'dense mass of people' as the boat train he was on pulled into Platform 14. Chaplin had to be carried through the roaring crowd towards a private car, as cries of 'Good old Charlie!' greeted him.

Charlie Chaplin, the local lad who was mobbed at Waterloo.

This event at Waterloo was perhaps one of the earliest demonstrations of the mania associated with celebrity culture. Chaplin would later be met with equal gusto on a return trip in 1952.

It was also announced that a new bar was to be unveiled towards the end of the year. The report was confident that when all was completed, 'Waterloo will be the finest railway station in the world'.

Amongst the last things to be reorganized were the office buildings, which were required for the ever-growing number of staff.

The very last public building to be opened was the Marble Hall buffet, which at 80ft (24m) long and nearly 40ft (12m) wide, was claimed to London's longest bar at the time. It also featured a modern coffee machine. It was open just in time for the Christmas rush, throwing its doors open to the public on 23 December 1921.

The new Waterloo now covered 24.5 acres (10ha) and contained twenty-one platforms, ranging in length from 530ft (160m) to 860ft (260m).

The Victory Arch

The crowning glory of the rebuilt Waterloo was the Victory Arch, which still provides the main entrance today.

The memorial was sculpted in Portland stone by Charles Edward Whiffen, for Farmer & Brindles; their workshop, based on Westminster Bridge Road, also created the carvings for the Albert Memorial and London's Natural History Museum. The son of a grocer, Whiffen was born in Cheltenham in 1867.

Waterloo Victory Arch.

Waterloo's clock.

He later moved to Fentiman Road, South Lambeth, and then to Altenburg Gardens in Battersea, where he died in 1929.

The memorial comprises several sections: at the top, above the sign for 'Waterloo Station', sits a statue of Britannia, bearing the torch of liberty. Below, curved around the archway itself, are seven round plaques, each of which bears the name of major theatres of war involved during World War I: Belgium, Italy, Dardanelles, France, Mesopotamia, Egypt and the North Sea.

On the left of the arch sits the demonic-faced figure of Bellona, the Roman goddess of war. On the right is Athena, goddess of courage and wisdom, who in this case also represents peace. Athena holds two items: a miniature figure of Nike, the winged goddess of victory, and a palm of peace. The names of all 585 L&SWR employees who were killed in the war, line the interior of the arch.

Waterloo Station's Clock

Waterloo's most famous timepiece is the four-sided clock that hangs above the main concourse – over a spot once occupied by the cab road during the days when vehicles were permitted to drive directly into the station. The clock was installed in the early 1920s by Gents of Leicester – who are still in business today – and has become a London landmark: 'Meet me under the clock' is a popular romantic phrase for couples seeking a rendezvous point in the bustling station.

Official Opening

After this mammoth project, which had taken some twenty years, the revamped Waterloo was finally ready for its official opening on the afternoon of 21 March 1922. The ceremony was to be conducted by King George V, but he was struck down by a cold that day. Therefore the task on that breezy, chilly day was handed to his wife, Queen Mary of Teck. The opening was captured on a brief, silent *Pathé News* reel (which can be found online), in which the Queen can be seen greeting a number of war veterans, then cutting the ribbon before a crowd of onlookers.

The Westminster Gazette stated there was something of an unreality about the opening, as the station had changed and regrown over two decades with barely any disruption to traffic. Nevertheless, they continued:

> *The symbolism of such an occasion is worthwhile. It embodies our recognition that in all the years of work there has been steady progress towards something complete, towards a real addition to the conveniences and beauty of London...*

Official opening of the new Waterloo, 1922.

CHAPTER 8

The 1920s, 1930s and World War II

On 16 June 1923, the *Westminster Gazette* observed the following episode:

> *In the tearoom at Waterloo Station the tall American gazed down in astonishment at the pink ice melting in its little paper cup.*
>
> *'Is that a full sized order?' he asked the waitress.*
>
> *'Yes, sir,' she said respectfully.*
>
> *'Say, sister, I wanted a plateful, not a tooth filling.'*

Apart from complaints about portion sizes, the new Waterloo station was met with almost universal praise, and as the Roaring Twenties settled into their stride, so too did the vastly expanded terminal.

Rather ironically, the L&SWR, which had done so much to forge the mighty new terminal, ceased to exist in 1923: under the Railways Act of 1921, it was merged with other companies to form the Southern Railway (which henceforth will be referred to as 'the Southern').

New additions continued to appear at the station throughout the early 1920s. In March 1922 a new W.H. Smith bookstall opened, followed in 1923 by a branch of Boots the chemist, and other shops. Another *Westminster Gazette* report, published just before Christmas 1923, described the station's new concourse as follows:

> *[It is] a remarkable shopping centre, which can now boast window displays equal to anything seen in Regent Street ...and in the last few months practically every kind of business – hosiers, grocers, chemists, tobacconists, fruiterers, hairdressers, tailors and athletic outfitters – has appeared.*

The same report also announced that a branch of the National Provincial and Union Bank was shortly due to open a branch at the station.

A row of telephone boxes was also installed, close to the mainline platforms, although these drew complaints for overcharging: at the time the official charge for a call within the London area (a radius of 10 miles) was 3d; the phones at Waterloo, however, charged 4d. This was apparently due to a loophole whereby the units were the property of Waterloo station, rather than the General Post Office.

A more interesting curiosity was an animated model of Bournemouth, which was installed in early 1935 as a means of drumming up business for the resort. As an advert in the press at the time described:

> *Televise Bournemouth at Waterloo station through the wonderful animated model – see the celebrated South Coast resort in every detail... the hotel where you wish to stay... Its proximity to*

the sea, amusement centres, gardens and parks.
Here is the whole town portrayed in miniature
and brought to London for your benefit.

WATERLOO STATION CINEMA

One of the most exciting additions to appear at Waterloo was its very own cinema, which opened on 27 August 1934. This cinema was established by British News Theatres Limited, who also ran a similar picture house at Victoria. As the company's name suggested, the cinema screened newsreels on a loop. Short documentaries and cartoons also featured, and in photographs of the building from the time, a cardboard cut-out of Mickey Mouse can be seen on the concourse, luring in viewers along with neon signs bearing the titles 'News Theatre' and 'News Interest, Cartoon Films'.

Designed by Alistair MacDonald – son of Prime Minister James Ramsay MacDonald, who had spent time studying skyscrapers in New York – the cinema's sleek, Art Deco frontage was situated on Waterloo's north-eastern side. Although the ticket booth was at ground level, the cinema itself was elevated and accessed via a staircase close to Platform 1. The auditorium, capable of seating 250 people, was a box-like structure that jutted out above Cab Road. An emergency staircase led down on the opposite side.

Location of Waterloo's former cinema, which was elevated above Cab Road. The concrete patch, seen in the brickwork on the left, marks the point where the emergency staircase exit was located.

Because of the cinema's compact nature, a new method of projection was employed, the Innes Projection System, which used an arrangement of mirrors; this was the first time it had been seen in the UK, and according to *The Times*:

> *...the 'false' distance gained by this method makes it possible to bring the front row of the seats to within a few feet of the mirror screen.*
> *Even so, there is no objectionable feeling of nearness or eye strain, as might be expected, because the mirror is not focused while*

Waterloo's cinema is visible in the background of this screenshot from The Terminus, 1961.

watching the performance – one looks beyond it. It is claimed that the system gives greater depth to the image...and that there is a considerable improvement in the quality of coloured films.

In October 1934, James Agate, writing for *The Tatler*, described a visit to the new picture house:

The Waterloo News Station has a fearsomely modern exterior; it suggests the kind of house admired aloofly in the glossiest and most expensive magazines, and it is distempered and illuminated in the most precious greens and lymphatic heliotropes. But once inside you have the familiar news fare.

Time is, as it should be, particularly in evidence. But it passed pleasantly on the screen – or it did in the hour I attended – with the delicate skill of Italian mosaic-workers, the wiles of rattle-snakes, the physiognomies of wine-tasters, the swiftness of Japanese errand-boys, the habits of the opossum, and the scenery of Iceland and of Northern Australia.

In December 1934, *The Stage* was full of praise for the cinema, in a snippet that reads: 'The little theatre at Waterloo Station is an ornate and very handy innovation. Make a point of missing a train, and help yourself to a bobsworth.'

In 1935, the company was rebranded Capital & Provincial News Theatres Ltd, and by 1953 their Waterloo branch was, at least according to the *Hampshire Telegraph and Post*, 'the best known of all News Theatres in this country'.

In 1938 the cinema was advertised as being open from Monday to Saturday, 11.30am to 11pm, and on Sundays from 5.30 to 11pm. Prices were 6d and 1s. Train arrival times, along with the platform number, could, if requested at the cashier box, be displayed on screen.

But with the increasing popularity of television in the 1950s and 1960s, viewers began to consume news reports in their own homes. In response, the cinema switched to screening vintage films under a new name: the 'Waterloo Station Classic.' Alan

Dent, writing for the *London Illustrated News* in December 1963, expressed his delight at the cinema's new repertory role, and after describing it as being 'cosy, clean and convenient', settled down to watch 1943's *Jane Eyre* starring Orson Welles and Joan Fontaine.

The cinema soldiered on until 14 March 1970, when, after screening an Alfred Hitchcock double bill, it closed its doors for good. The building was demolished in 1988.

EARLY TELEVISION

One intriguing aspect about Waterloo in the 1930s was that it offered passengers the opportunity to view early television broadcasts.

The cost of television sets during this era was astronomical, the equivalent today to the price of a new car. Naturally this put this state-of-the-art technology out of the reach of all but the very wealthy. However, from the late summer of 1936, the travelling public – provided they had a valid railway ticket – could view this new-fangled device in the waiting room at Waterloo station.

The set used was a 14in screen, walnut-panelled Baird Type T5. It was named after its inventor, John Logie Baird, who had been tirelessly developing television at his lab on Soho's Frith Street since the early 1920s, and it was the world's first 405-line high-definition receiver. No doubt due to its high value – it was priced at 85 guineas – the set was surrounded by a waist-high metal bar, which also prevented anyone from leaning over, and prying hands fiddling with the dials.

When first installed in August 1936, the set broadcast a test transmission from Radiolympia (which, as the name suggests, came from the Olympia Exhibition Hall). According to *The Times*, during this period of experimental broadcasts, over 8,000 people managed to view the set at Waterloo – and when, in the autumn of that same year, the BBC began a regular programme of broadcasting from Alexandra Palace, the set at Waterloo was on hand to televise them. The set-up was described in *The Nottingham Journal*:

Advertisement for a Baird T5 set, the type of model installed in Waterloo's waiting room.

The Southern Railway are introducing regular television programmes at Waterloo Station, London. Every weekday except Saturdays, the programme broadcast from Alexandra Palace will be shown in the waiting room opposite No. 16 platform from 11am to 12 noon and from 3pm to 4pm. Admission is free, but restricted to the holders of railway tickets (including season tickets).

These brief show times reflected the broadcast limitations of the day. The morning slot would have shown a test transmission film of some nature. Then after a close-down, the BBC would begin their variety of programmes at 3pm. To pick a day at random – let's say, 17 November 1936 – this is what you would have been able to view had you been in Waterloo's waiting room (as listed in *The Radio Times*):

15.00: Programme Summary
15.05: Inn Signs Through the Ages
15.20: Film
15.35: Interval. Time, Weather

15.40: Starlight. With Leonard Henry, Comedian.
16.00 Close. At the close of this afternoon's programme a chart arranged in co-operation with the Air Ministry will forecast the weather.

Waterloo's waiting room was closed in the evening, meaning the set was unable to broadcast the later schedule, which commenced at 9pm.

As well as providing a venue where people could view broadcasts, Waterloo station itself appeared on television in May 1939 when the BBC transmitted live footage of the King and Queen at the station as they prepared to embark upon a state visit to Canada.

Waterloo appeared again the following month when the royal couple returned. As a listing from the time described: '5.15 – London's Welcome to the King and Queen on their return from their State Visit to North America, as seen at Waterloo station…'.

The BBC's first era of regular television programmes came to an end on 1 September 1939 when it abruptly went off air following fears the transmissions could be exploited by Nazi bombers.

Further entertainment commenced at Waterloo in September 1937 when the station's loudspeakers began to pipe canned music to commuters, an innovation that *The Bystander* rather sarcastically described as 'a pleasing idea on the part of the railways to sing to the weary serfs of the Machine Age'.

The music was designed to reflect the time of day: in the morning rush hour it was full of pomp, whilst the evening equivalent tended to be more relaxing. Waterloo's tinny muzak remained a feature at the station for many decades.

WORLD WAR II

World War II was expected some time before it finally erupted in early September 1939. Consequently, Waterloo was witness to a number of events that were a prelude to the conflict. For example, in November 1938, a stall was erected on the concourse by the Auxiliary Air Force for the purpose of encouraging men aged between twenty-five and fifty to sign up as barrage balloon operators.

The following year, the deterioration of international events was made explicit when on 21 June, 287 Jewish refugees arrived at Waterloo after a long and exhausting voyage aboard the *St Louis*. The ship had travelled to Cuba and the USA, where it was turned away in both instances. After sailing back across the Atlantic, Britain along with France, Belgium and Holland each agreed to take in a percentage of passengers. *The Times* reported on their arrival at Waterloo the following day:

> *Tears of relief stood in the refugees' eyes as they stepped on to the platform to be greeted warmly by their friends and guarantors and to receive the bunches of flowers which their English friends had brought with them. More than 40 small children, many of them babies in arms, were with the party.*

In August 1939 and with war now just weeks away, a blackout was implemented. At this stage, *The Times* reported that, looking from the roof of Shell Mex House, 'the blackout was by no means complete. Lights inside Waterloo station could be seen as a faint glow, and outside the station there was a bright group of lights.'

This ineffective cloak was soon remedied: Waterloo's vast glass roof was painted black, whilst the concourse and platforms below were bathed in a dim, eerie blue light. If an air-raid was in progress, an overhead red light would be lit as a warning. In the daytime, this made the terminus a gloomy place; speaking in 1996, journalist Alistair Cooke described the station at that time as 'dark as a catacomb'.

Meanwhile, the steps outside the main entrance were painted in a chequered black and white pattern for the dual purpose of camouflaging them whilst giving the public a rough idea as to where to tread. Later, during the spring of 1942, experimental fluorescent markings (powered by ultra-violet lights) were trialled on handrails at the main entrance, on the stairs down to the Bakerloo line, along the road crossing between the main station and Waterloo Junction (now Waterloo East), and above the telephones sign and the cab exit.

Staff air-raid shelter (to the right) beneath Waterloo.

Beneath the station, part of the network of supporting arches was converted into an air-raid shelter for the use of staff. As in World War I, part of the same area was also used as a secure storage area for government documents.

TROOP MOVEMENTS AT WATERLOO

Once Britain had declared war on Germany, Waterloo was thrown into the task of transporting countless military personnel, just as it had done in World War I. One of the first groups to pass through Waterloo were 1,600 Frenchmen who were resident in Great Britain, but had been recalled home to fight. As *The Times* reported:

> *These men represented all classes of workers. There were young clergymen, onion sellers from Brittany who had been in this country for only a few weeks, actors, journalists, waiters and students. Wives were among the many who had come to see them off, and there were affecting farewell scenes.*

For this send-off, the French Ambassador was in attendance, and it was reported that crowds at the station cheered the men on, along with shouts of 'Vive la France!' and 'Vive l'Angleterre!'

Similar scenes were detailed in *The Times* in April 1940, when a detachment of the 1st Canadian Division arrived at the station, upon which they were given 'a warm and friendly welcome' before marching to Wellington Barracks. The same report described Waterloo as it appeared under wartime conditions:

In the changed conditions of war the station was alive with the movement of troops, parties of men from every branch of the fighting forces going about their duties. Civilians pausing to watch the arrival of the Canadians found themselves standing beside other soldiers from Canada, from New Zealand, and from other parts of the Empire.

A great cheer of welcome was raised by the crowd as the detachment began its march along the platform with fixed bayonets, led by the band of the Grenadier Guards and the pipers of the Irish Guards, both in khaki.

Outside the station people stood crowded along the pavements, and as the detachment reached them, many fell in and marched beside it. It was a simple but stirring incident in the war-time life of London.

In the same month, the public were given a further insight into the war when a mobile railway workshop, built by the Ministry of Supply for use by the British Expeditionary Force in France, was displayed at the station. The unit consisted of three covered vans packed with tools, stores and equipment, and modified to deal with the requirements of French railways.

The following month, just a few weeks before the events at Dunkirk, refugees from Belgium and the Netherlands arrived at Waterloo, all of whom 'had pitiful stories to tell of the ordeals they had suffered'.

In August 1940, Waterloo's speakers began to pipe music for longer periods, now between 9am and 9pm. According to *The Daily Herald*, this was so that 'people shall be able to see off their relatives in the services in a cheerful atmosphere'.

As in World War I, the YMCA established a canteen, along with a lounge and recreation area, at Waterloo to serve the men and women of the armed forces. This opened on 10 September 1939 between platforms 15 and 16, and was soon serving several thousands of people a day.

The Union Jack Club opposite Waterloo was also on hand, and in the summer of 1940 an annexe was opened to deal with the extra demand – between September 1939 and June 1940 it was said that no fewer than 162,284 members of the forces – 'including 16,000 from the Dominions and Colonies' – had slept at the club, with even more using the facilities during the daytime.

Despite this, the facilities did sometimes struggle to cope with the sheer number of personnel. In January 1944, *The Daily Mirror* provided a portrait of Waterloo's overcrowded conditions:

The steady snoring from the dark benches ceased for a few seconds as the policeman went round calling 'Anyone for the 1.25?' He shook the huddled figures – stranded soldiers and sailors – telling them that it was 12.15 and they had better start to queue, as the throng was already four abreast and eighty yards long.

It was Sunday night at Waterloo station, London, and the end of week-end leave. Every week-end hundreds of soldiers and sailors are stranded. With gas masks as pillows, papers as blankets, and hard benches as beds they wait for an early morning train. These men were weary and cold. Many were hungry. The hostels around were full. Even the floor of the warm waiting room was packed.

UNDER ATTACK

Being a major railway hub, it was inevitable that Waterloo would be targeted. In preparation, huge steel floodgates were installed on the Bakerloo line, with sets at both Waterloo and Charing Cross. These were in place by the autumn of 1938, and first rolled shut on 3 September 1939 following the false air-raid alert that occurred just eight minutes after Neville Chamberlain's infamous radio broadcast announcing that Britain was now at war with Germany.

Portraits of an Evacuation

With the threat of air attack, many children were also on the move, and Waterloo handled a great many of these young evacuees early in the war. In the first three days of this huge operation, 12,700 children passed through the station, many of whom had been transported to the terminus by trams, buses and tube trains.

Troops and evacuees at Waterloo. Note: in the background it is possible to spot the emergency staircase connected to the old News Cinema.

On 1 September 1939, BBC correspondent Seymour July de Lotbinière reported directly from Waterloo's platform 12 as the evacuation commenced. His sixteen-minute radio piece featuring observations, interviews, the sound of steam engines, and a group of children cheerfully singing 'The Lambeth Walk', was broadcast across both the Empire and the USA. It can be heard today via the BBC's archive.

A more lighthearted description of the evacuation from Waterloo appears in Norman Collins' 1945 novel, *London Belongs to Me.* In the scene, Connie – an elderly and slightly eccentric nightclub employee – heads to Waterloo to witness the exodus because 'it wasn't every day that there was drama like that going on just around the corner.' The scene continues:

She got to the station at about 10.30. At first it was difficult to get in because there was so much happening. But she managed it all right in the end, even though it did mean having a few words over her shoulder with a policeman.

And once inside, what a scene it was! Not a bit what she'd imagined it, mind you. No screaming, no hysteria, no panic. Just rows and rows of children, each with a gas-mask, a parcel containing rations and sponge-bag, and a label to prove that the child really was itself and not a totally different child from some other school...

The teachers who were looking after these enormous families might have been in charge of a mass visit to the Zoo. They merely had about them that look of depressed watchfulness which is common to all adults accompanying school outings. The children themselves were blithe, excited and ready for anything.

Floodgates were also installed on the Northern line at Waterloo, each of which were 13in (33cm) thick and weighed 6 tons. It was claimed the barriers could resist a force of over 800 tons.

The most direct hits on Waterloo occurred on the station's north-western sidings, the location of which is now occupied by the former Eurostar terminal. The primary damage occurred in a series of attacks focused on the railway approaches themselves. One of these, as seen in Chapter 4, destroyed the Necropolis station on Westminster Bridge Road. When damage did occur, repairs were carried out fairly rapidly, although the terminal had to close for a brief period when a fire raid targeted Waterloo with oil bombs and incendiaries.

Raging fires caused by explosives landing nearby were a continual threat to the terminal, with the worst blaze occurring on the night of the 10–11 May 1940. This event was described in *The Times*, some time after the event in November 1943:

Outside the station many fires were raging, while inside more bombs were falling. One high explosive fell on the track, and a fire started in the stores. A fire bomb fell on the premises adjoining the workshops and started a fire which quickly spread from the parcels vans to a stock of spirits which was soon a furnace. The next morning the contents of two more stores burst into flames, the bricks were white-hot and many were dropping away. Trains were moved from the danger zone.

In December 1940, one air raid successfully targeted the main entrance, leaving a large crater in the road.

Throughout the Blitz, a Union Jack flag was flown high above the station and suffered considerable damage as a result. The following year, this symbol made its way to the British Railways' Offices in New York City, where the proud yet tattered flag was displayed in the window.

Later in the war, Waterloo was also witness to V1 rockets. On the 23 June 1943 one such V1 exploded directly outside Waterloo, close to the main entrance on York Road. The ensuing blast killed six people, destroyed railway offices, 110ft (33.5m) of track and an eight-car train. The roof and top deck of two buses were also torn off.

A week later, on the afternoon of the 30th, the ominous warbling of another V1 cut out as it flew above the terminal. The rocket plummeted over the Thames and smashed into Aldwych, killing forty-six people and injuring at least 200.

On 4 January 1945 Waterloo Station narrowly escaped a strike from Hitler's second 'vengeance' weapon: the supersonic V2. This terrifying missile exploded approximately half a mile away on Morton Place, off Cosser Street. Forty-two victims perished in the blast.

During World War II, 626 Southern Railway employees lost their lives, and a plaque honouring their memory was added to the Waterloo's entrance arch. A further plaque, commemorating railway employees who gave their lives on D-Day, was added on 6 June 1994 as a way of marking the 50th anniversary.

CHAPTER 9

Post-War Waterloo

When VE Day arrived in May 1945, Waterloo could be proud of the role it had served in the war. And after six years of handling military traffic, it was now time to prepare for an influx of holidaymakers who were understandably keen, after much hardship, to travel to the seaside for some sun and relaxation. The weekend of the 14–15 July 1945 was particularly busy, with around 200,000 travellers crowding into the station. So packed were some carriages that *The Sunday Mirror* reported that 'railway officials had to help passengers climb out through the windows'. As a result, Waterloo had to put on an extra twenty-eight trains – no mean feat considering the recent ravages of war.

Despite victory in Europe, the war was still, of course, raging in the Pacific, and even after World War II finally ended there were still countless troop movements to facilitate. In September 1945, MP Sir Edward Salt wrote to *The Times* to express his concern at the conditions in which service personnel were required to wait at Waterloo. His account told of a naval friend who had 'arrived at Waterloo Station at 11.50pm, where he found a queue that had already been started for the 2.40am train which

he had to catch to get back to his depot by 6am.' He continued:

This queue was in an underground passage, frightfully hot and stuffy, with the doubtful advantage that you could not fall down, even if you wanted, owing to being packed tight. Several fainted, and when the gates were opened at 2.30am everyone started to push. One of the main troubles was to keep your feet on the ground and not be shot out of the crowd like a piece of soap.

Disused pedestrian subway beneath Waterloo.

Salt also claimed that one fellow was crushed against a gate, resulting in three broken ribs. He concluded:

> *I am informed that similar conditions to those described herein are not uncommon, and remembering the tragic episode of a London shelter, I hope the railway authorities will have an immediate inquiry into the whole question and take suitable action.*

The 'tragic episode of a London shelter' to which Salt referred was 1943's Bethnal Green disaster, in which 173 civilians perished after being crushed to death on the staircase leading into the tube station.

A response from Southern's Public Relations Officer, C. Grasemann, appeared in the paper the following day, in which he claimed the subterranean queues were formed on the insistence of the naval and military authorities. Although he admitted there had been other complaints from the public, Grasemann also stated that 'Inquiry of men in the queues had been specially made, and in each case they said they had no objection to it…'.

By autumn 1945, emaciated prisoners of war were returning from Japan, and Waterloo was on hand to receive them. On 8 October RMS *Corfu* docked in Southampton with 500 such men and women, who were taken by special train to Waterloo. At the terminal, a number of children eagerly stood by the gates to catch a glimpse of the fathers they knew only from photographs. Despite the fanfare surrounding this event, certain details in the press revealed the horrific conditions to which the POWs had been subjected; at least one of the arrivals had to be carried away by stretcher, 'unable to speak'.

In January 1946 Waterloo took part in what some later dubbed 'Operation Diaper': the emigration of 500 British women who had married American servicemen during the war. Aided by the Women's Voluntary Service, a special 'Bride Train' for the wives and children of the GIs was put on at Waterloo for the first leg of a journey that would eventually reach the USA and a reunion with their sweethearts.

100th ANNIVERSARY

The year 1948 marked Waterloo's centenary, an event celebrated with a week-long exhibition at the station. On display were prints of Lambeth Marsh as it had appeared before the railways' arrival, early timetables, and a number of photographs taken throughout the terminal's history. Two vintage Box Hill locomotives also made an appearance, and the atmosphere was further enhanced by people turning up in period costume.

Interestingly, *The Times* reported that amongst the few relics to survive from the old Waterloo were the station's bell and 'the toll house near Griffin Street, where the police collected tolls from the cabmen coming into the station.' Griffin Street, which was located on the south-western side of the station, is now long lost; sadly one must assume that the toll booth was swept away with it.

By this point, numerous bomb craters pitted around Waterloo were beginning to sprout clusters of bracken and flowers. One correspondent writing for *The Times* suggested there was some irony to this, as Waterloo had been built close to the once very popular Cuper's Pleasure Gardens, and called to mind a song that referenced them:

> *Twas down in Cupid's Garden,*
> *For the pleasure I did go*
> *All for to see the flowers*
> *That in the garden grow.*

A booklet by H.G. Davis entitled *Waterloo Station Centenary*, priced at 1s 6d, was also published to coincide with the event. The cover featured illustrations by Helen McKie depicting two locomotives, one from 1848 and one from 1948.

THE COADE STONE LION

In 1951, Waterloo gained a mascot: the Coade stone lion. Weighing 13 tonnes, the sculpture was created in 1837 by Warwickshire-born artist, William Frederick Woodington. The material used was Coade stone, a special recipe formulated in the late eighteenth century by Eleanor Coade; the stone is famously impervious to the effects of pollution.

The Coade stone lion.

The lion – which was one of two and originally painted red – initially stood high above the gateway to the Lion Brewery on Belvedere Road, a site now occupied by the Royal Festival Hall. It was a popular artwork; one admirer was Emile Zola, who in later life made a special trip to London just to view what he affectionately referred to as 'my lion' one last time.

Following the demolition of the brewery in 1949, King George VI insisted the lion be saved, and it was decided the stone beast would be well suited to a new location outside Waterloo – after all, the recently nationalized British Railways now had a lion as their corporate logo. The lion was situated close to the

Victory Arch steps, on the junction of Cab Road, from where it peered out across York Road.

It remained in place until 1966, when it was removed to make way for the large Elizabeth House office block. It was re-sited on Westminster Bridge, where it remains today. Its counterpart can be seen outside Twickenham Rugby stadium.

THE FESTIVAL OF BRITAIN

The placement of the lion outside Waterloo coincided with a major post-war event that ran in the summer of 1951: the Festival of Britain. The main showpiece for this nation-wide event, designed to boost morale in the aftermath of World War II, occurred on the South Bank, just moments away from Waterloo, and featured, amongst many things, the Dome of Discovery, the Royal Festival Hall, and a sleek futuristic artwork known as 'The Skylon'.

The ticket office was situated outside Waterloo, beside the Coade stone lion. Also near the entrance stood an 8ft (2.4m) tall, specially commissioned artwork sculpted by Mitzi Cunliff called *Root Bodied Forth*. The current whereabouts of this sculpture, which featured an entwined, figurative couple, is now a mystery. Elsewhere, one of the walls inside Waterloo's entrance was decorated with colourful children's handprints.

As well as serving as a main entry point for the exhibition, Waterloo also provided a base for the

The Festival of Britain site, 1951.

Festival's control room, which was located above the terminal's entrance. At the height of the exhibition, a journalist from *The Yorkshire Post and Leeds Mercury* was granted a tour:

I penetrated today one of the South Bank's secret haunts – the Control Centre of the Exhibition above the Waterloo Station entrance. There, Mr Norman MacDermott, the General Manager, showed me some of the mysterious machines that keep a second-by-second check on attendance figures and otherwise perform electrical miracles unknown to visitors.

If by ill-luck a fire occurred within the Exhibition, or a serious accident took place, or a crime were perpetrated, no general alarm would sound. A secret code of light or sound signals would be flashed to appropriate officials and the necessary localised action would be taken without the general body of patrons having the least idea that anything untoward had occurred.

Waterloo Scrub

The coronation of Her Majesty Queen Elizabeth II took place in 1953, and in the months leading up to this historic event the nation's railways were given some heavy duty cleaning. It was reported in *The Nottingham Journal* that:

...the biggest window-cleaning job in London is reckoned to be at Waterloo Station. It has taken five men three months to clean the 22,400 squares of glass forming the roof, the total area of which is about 13 acres.

WATERLOO AIR TERMINAL

For a period in the 1950s, Waterloo station was closely connected with air travel. The idea of combining Waterloo with aviation wasn't a new one. In the 1920s and 1930s it had been suggested, rather outlandishly,

that a landing strip could be placed on top of the terminal's roof.

In April 1930, the Southern's General Manager, Herbert Walker, addressed a parliamentary committee tasked with examining the possibility of placing an aerodrome in central London. Walker disclosed that 'tentative plans' had once been drawn up for the demolition of Waterloo's glass roof, which would then have been replaced with 'a great concrete floor supported by steel stanchions driven deep into the London clay'. However, it was clear that as well as blocking out all light into the station, such a landing platform would not have been big or strong enough, not to mention presenting the danger of low-flying aircraft to nearby homes and other buildings.

In 1953 a more realistic air connection came to fruition: the British European Airways (BEA) Waterloo air terminal, a three-storey handling centre designed for transporting air passengers to the then fledgling London Airport (better known today, of course, as Heathrow) and Northolt. The BEA terminal was designed to replace the much smaller Kensington air station, which, although closer to the airports, could only handle 7,000 people daily. In comparison, Waterloo's could process 16,000 passengers per day.

Waterloo air terminal was located opposite the station, beside the London Underground entrance on York Road, on land recently vacated by the Festival of Britain. It contained facilities for checking in and dropping off baggage, as well as a modest restaurant and lounge area. There was also a small car

Site of the BEA terminal, which was located beside the tube station entrance.

park towards the rear. Once passengers had been processed, they were taken to London Airport by a fleet of thirty-seven-seater coaches. At the time, this service linking central London to the airport was vital, as other transport options were then very limited.

The terminal – described by some press reports as being the world's most modern – was officially opened on 21 May 1953 by the Minister of Transport, A.T. Lennox-Boyd, with the words: 'We meet on the eve of a great air age. The number of scheduled movements has doubled in the last four years, and looks like doubling again before 1960.'

BEA's chairman, Lord Douglas of Kirtleside, was also on hand to offer some words: 'I hope before long we shall have a helicopter station here, possibly on the roof of Waterloo Station.'

The idea of flying helicopters from Waterloo was indeed under consideration. A few months prior to the air terminal opening, John Profumo – then parliamentary secretary to the Ministry of Civil Aviation – made a test flight from the South Bank as part of an exploration into securing a heliport site. After buzzing over Waterloo, Charing Cross and the Houses of Parliament, Profumo declared the experience to be 'the best thing on earth', a comment that

The Daily Herald wryly described as his 'enthusiasm getting the better of accuracy'.

After the flight, Profumo said the South Bank was the best site, although he admitted noise would be a potential problem. Lambeth Council agreed about the noise issue, and suggested a helicopter pad could perhaps be constructed instead in the middle of the Thames, possibly over Hungerford Bridge. A helicopter service was indeed inaugurated in 1954, with the landing pad located on ground close to the BEA terminal. This was achieved via new regulations permitting helicopters to fly at a minimum of 500ft (152m) above the Thames, and to land or take off close to Waterloo, provided twenty-four hours' notice was given.

The first flight landed on 18 June: a Westland S55, which had flown from Yeovil carrying Westland's Sales Manager, Harold Penrose. On the same day, another three helicopters used the site, making thirteen landings between them. Soon a service was offering direct helicopter transfer between Waterloo and London Airport, a journey that by air took just thirteen minutes. The service was priced at 30s for a single flight.

Despite these innovations, the BEA air terminal was shortlived. It ceased operating in early October 1957, and was replaced by the new West London BEA terminal near Earls Court. Both of these centres are now long demolished: the Waterloo terminal was swept away to make room for the Shell Tower, whilst the West London centre has since been replaced by a supermarket and apartments.

BEA bus.

1950s Celebrities at Waterloo

With the jet-age fast approaching, the 1950s were the last true decade in which crowds of fans could catch a glimpse of their favourite American film and music stars at Waterloo as they arrived or departed from boat trains.

In September 1956, Liberace arrived at Waterloo where he was 'mobbed by a screaming, shrieking crowd of over 3,000 women…Dozens of policemen linked arms in an effort to stop the crowds swarming over the crush barriers at Waterloo Station.' Many fans managed to barge through the police and proceeded to wave flowers at their hero. *The Daily Mirror* reported that the famous pianist smiled constantly as he made his way through the station, even at an opposition group of students carrying a banner which said: WE HATE LIBERACE…CHARLIE KUNZ FOREVER.

Similar scenes occurred the following February when Bill Hayley of 'Rock Around the Clock' fame steamed into Waterloo and was met by what *The London Illustrated News* called 'a surging mass of youths' and 'mass hysteria'. In the scuffle, policemen lost hats, and teenagers who'd come to see the American rock-and-roll pioneer risked being crushed against the gates. As *The Times* noted: 'Mr Haley now knows how London teenagers can welcome an idol.'

Other famous faces to pass through Waterloo in the 1950s included Rita Hayworth, Buster Keaton – who refused to smile for the camera – and local hero Charlie Chaplin, who was received just as raucously as he had been in the 1920s.

THE WINDRUSH GENERATION

On 22 June 1948 the *Empire Windrush* docked at Tilbury, which meant that its pioneering group of 492 West Indian migrants made the onward journey to London via Liverpool Street. But over the following years – well into the 1960s – most of those travelling to the UK from the Caribbean sailed into Southampton, from where they would catch the boat train to Waterloo; thus the terminal was intrinsically linked with the Windrush Generation.

Waterloo's role during this period is atmospherically captured in the opening to the 1956 novel *The Lonely Londoners*, by Trinidad-born author Sam Selvon. Written in a style that reflects a mixture of Caribbean dialects, the book opens with the main character, Moses Aloetta, who, in a choking London fog, catches a bus to Waterloo where he has agreed to meet a friend of a friend who is due in on the boat train:

Windrush arrivals at Waterloo from the 1961 film, Terminus.

When he [Moses] get to Waterloo he hop off and went in the station and right away in that big station he had a feeling of homesickness that he never felt in the nine-ten years he in this country.

For the old Waterloo is a place of arrival and departure, is a place where you see people crying goodbye and kissing welcome, and he hardly have time to sit down on a bench before this feeling of nostalgia hit him and he was surprise…. It was here that Moses did land when he come to London, and he have no doubt that when the time come, if it ever come, it would be here he would say goodbye to the big city.

Selvon also mentions that it wasn't uncommon for people such as Moses to pop to Waterloo whenever a boat train was due in:

They like to see the familiar faces, they like to watch their countrymen coming off the train, and sometimes they might spot somebody they know: 'Aye Watson! What the hell you doin' in Brit'n boy?'

There were occasions when the arrival of boat trains carrying people from the West Indies attracted unwanted attention. On 1 September 1960, for instance, a group of twenty young men from an early incarnation of the British National Party gathered at Waterloo to wave posters and shout racist slogans. They were escorted from the station by the British Transport Police, although they made several attempts to force their way back.

In June 2019 it was announced by Baroness Floella Benjamin – who herself arrived in the UK via Waterloo in 1960 – that a memorial honouring the Windrush Generation would soon be placed at the terminal. This decision created some controversy, however, with the Windrush Foundation suggesting that such a memorial would be better suited to Windrush Square in Brixton.

FAREWELL TO WINSTON

On 24 January 1965, Sir Winston Churchill passed away at the age of ninety. Six days later, on 30 January, his state funeral – the first to occur in the twentieth century for a politician – was held, with Waterloo playing a key role. On that cold morning, Churchill's funeral procession left Westminster Hall and proceeded along Whitehall and The Strand, towards St Paul's Cathedral. It then passed through the City – Cannon Street, Eastcheap and the Tower, where the coffin was placed on a boat and taken back along the Thames to Festival Hall pier.

From there, the draped coffin was carried along the South Bank, crossing Belvedere Road and York Road, its journey finally ending at Waterloo station

Battle of Britain Class Pacific 34051, which hauled Churchill's funeral train in 1965.

where the procession entered via Cab Road, beneath Waterloo's clock.

At Waterloo, Churchill's coffin was borne by young soldiers serving with his old cavalry regiment, who placed it on a train – made up of six Pullman coaches, including a special bogie car for the coffin – at Platform 11. Footage of Churchill's funeral procession was broadcast live by the BBC, until it left Waterloo.

The engine tasked with hauling the funeral service was a Battle of Britain Class steam engine – number 34051 – named, rather appropriately, *Winston Churchill*, a title it had received in 1947. The driver, sixty-one-year-old A.W. Hurley, had worked as a fireman on a train that had carried Churchill in 1941 between Southampton and Surbiton – it had been unable to make it to Waterloo due to bomb damage.

The engine is now held by the National Railway Museum, as is the funeral car, which returned to the UK in 2007 after spending forty years in California.

1960s Innovations

Throughout the 1960s, a number of improvements appeared at Waterloo. These included a 'Directomat', installed in 1965 and capable of providing printed information in answer to any of 120 questions; 'Autoslot Mark 3' ticket machines on the Waterloo & City line (which replaced the manned booking offices); and in 1967, a 'newscaster' – a 64ft (19.5m) long screen that displayed advertisements between 8am and midnight. Similar to the device used at Piccadilly Circus, the newscaster was capable of displaying four colours and was positioned above the old news cinema.

By the 1960s, Waterloo was also the proud owner of the largest, privately owned automatic telephone exchange: it had 1,600 lines and was based in a modern building overlooking Lower Marsh.

Outside the station, in 1962 a 'Panda crossing' was trialled, essentially a zebra crossing but with pedestrian-controlled lights. It was not a success.

In 1979, Waterloo would participate in an equally sombre funeral: that of Lord Mountbatten, who was killed in an IRA terrorist attack.

WATERLOO SUNSET

Although suburban services had been electrified in the early twentieth century, mainline steam services continued to serve Waterloo for decades, and the station ended up being the last London terminus to accommodate them.

The last steam service to pull into Waterloo was the 14.09 from Weymouth, hauled by a Merchant Navy Pacific Class, no. 35030, named *Elder Dempster Lines*,

Merchant Navy Class Ellerman Lines *at Nine Elms, 1959. This engine can now be seen at the National Railway Museum, where it has been adapted to display the internal workings of a steam engine.*

Locomotive 41298 at Waterloo, 1967. This engine is preserved by the Isle of Wight Steam Railway.

Steam locomotive approaching Waterloo, March 1965.

SR Merchant Navy Class 35028 at Waterloo, 2009.

on the afternoon of Sunday 9 July 1967, with farewell messages chalked over its smokebox door. Later that evening, the last steam engine departed Waterloo: a British Railways Standard Class 3, number 77014 pulling a van train to Bournemouth.

Steam made a welcome return to Waterloo in July 2019 with a regular schedule of summer excursions: the Royal Windsor Steam Express, and in the evening, the Sunset Express.

CONCOURSE PR

A common sight at Waterloo Station in the late 1960s and early 1970s were the various publicity events for certain companies and tourist boards that took over the concourse. In January 1967, for example, Scottish tourism was promoted for two weeks. The terminal was bedecked in flags and bunting, Scottish music was played from the station's loudspeakers, traditional dancers and bagpipers demonstrated their skills, and daily haggis-eating contests were held. To top it all, a huge dry ski-slope was also installed.

Later that year, the Welsh Tourist Board took over the concourse for a fortnight: daffodils were handed out, models of red dragons were dotted everywhere, and Welsh music was played. The centrepiece was a model of a mountain, complete with dripping water. Welsh laverbread was also handed out to commuters.

In 1970 it was the turn of the Isle of Man: an exhibition stand sold the island's unique 50-pence note, despite the Bank of England's warning that it was not legal tender. Mr G. Andrews, of the Manx Tourist Board, commented: 'People seem to like it better than the 50 penny piece. Our notes are selling like hot cakes.'

In April 1970, there was a swimming-pool exhibition, and the following year, the 14,000,000th Volkswagen Beetle to be built was proudly displayed on the concourse for a fortnight. Then in 1972, Pan Am pushed their public relations at Waterloo by unveiling a full-sized mock-up of a Boeing 747 cabin.

Advertising for an institution closer to home, Chessington Zoo, proved somewhat problematic, however, as there were at least two instances when the stuffed

Waterloo interior Cab Road, 1974.

animals (namely a tiger and a chimpanzee) were stolen. In both cases the thieves were caught and charged.

In April 1974, shortly after winning the Eurovision song contest (held that year at The Dome in Brighton), Swedish supergroup ABBA took part in a photo shoot at the station – rather fitting considering they had won the contest with their song 'Waterloo'…

SOCIAL STRIFE

Throughout the 1970s and 1980s Waterloo and the area surrounding the terminal gained a reputation as being a dangerous locality. In part this image was driven by a number of shocking murders that occurred during those decades.

The first case was that of sixty-eight-year-old Graham Arthur Hills, a retired railway clerk who was stabbed in the heart on 15 August 1972 after being mugged by a gang of three young men. The assault took place on the footbridge over York Road as Mr Hills was heading to Waterloo to return to his home in Barnes after spending a night at the opera. Three youths aged seventeen, sixteen and fifteen were charged with his killing.

Another shocking incident occurred on 14 May 1970 when a speeding car appeared to lose control at the station and hurtled towards a large crowd of people. A railway policeman named Ron Aston bravely stood in the vehicle's path, waving his arms to alert pedestrians before leaping on to the vehicle's bonnet. Unfortunately he was unable to stop the car from hitting and killing thirty-one-year-old Gordon Mackie. Gordon was a music conductor, and the following day he had been due to conduct the Royal Liverpool Philharmonic Orchestra in what would have been a defining moment in his career.

Waterloo, December 1975.

Air-raid siren on the Waterloo East–
Charing Cross line. Little is known about
this siren; it is most likely post 1945,
installed to warn against flooding and,
more chillingly, nuclear attack.

A Great Train Robber at Waterloo

From 1975 onwards, Ronald Christopher Edwards – aka 'Buster', and one of those found guilty of robbing the Glasgow to London Royal Mail train in 1963 – was a regular fixture at Waterloo. Following his release, Buster became a florist and set up his stall just outside the station, beside the Underground entrance on Waterloo Road. Interestingly, Waterloo had itself played a part in the robbery, as it was at the station's buffet that Buster had liaised with Tommy Wisbey and Roger Cordrey, a meeting in which the underworld figures agreed to work together on the heist.

Buster worked his patch until November 1994. Then on the 28th of that month he was found dead, hanging from a noose in a lock-up garage on Greet Street, close to Waterloo East station.

On 25 October 1980 police constable and father of four, Frank O'Neil, was murdered outside Waterloo station by a drug addict named Josun Soan. The attack took place after Soan attempted to secure drugs with a forged prescription, which he presented in Boots the chemist on Lower Marsh.

When approached by police, Soan – who was hallucinating on drugs – claimed he thought PC O'Neil was a bear: 'I saw it out of the corner of my eye, which scared the living daylights out of me...I got a knife out and slashed in that direction' he would later say in court.

As PC O'Neil lay bleeding, his colleague, twenty-five-year-old Angela Seeds, gave chase, and along with a colleague named Ken Fletcher who had responded to a radio call for help, managed to apprehend Soan outside Lambeth North tube station. Soan was later found guilty and sentenced to life. An office complex on Clapham Road was later named in Frank O'Neil's honour.

Later in the decade, on 9 December 1988 – just days before the Clapham rail disaster – thirty-five-year-old Scotsman John Heron was stabbed to death whilst queuing for a ticket. Despite an appeal on the BBC programme *Crimewatch*, his attacker was never identified.

Since the 1960s, Waterloo and its environs had drawn in many of the capital's homeless people seeking shelter at night on the station's benches. By the 1980s, a community dubbed 'Cardboard City' had evolved throughout the subterranean passageways surrounding the station. At its height, it was estimated that some 200 people were sleeping rough around Waterloo. In April 1989, one correspondent, worried about the impact the area would have on travellers to the proposed Channel Tunnel terminal (*see* Chapter 10) penned a bitter letter – displaying sentiments akin to Victorian scorn – to *The Times* to voice their concerns about the situation:

> *It stinks, it is pathetic, it is frightening and it is getting worse every day. The socio-political explanations for the growth of this cardboard village are no doubt as complex and varied as are individual backgrounds of the bag ladies, the meths drinkers and the teenage beggars who inhabit it.*

Cardboard City was controversially swept away in the late 1990s to make way for the IMAX cinema, which now dominates the large 'bull ring' roundabout outside the station.

THE LATE TWENTIETH CENTURY

Although not on the same scale as the 1920s and 1930s, Waterloo continued to receive improvements and new concepts throughout the 1970s and 1980s. In 1978 three modern Swiss-designed ticket machines were trialled at the station. They proved unpopular, however, as they were slow and unable to accept the new £1 note. Then in 1980, Waterloo became the site of the first Casey Jones burger bar, an innovation by British Rail to compete with the burgeoning American fast-food market.

In the mid-1980s, the station's archaic lavatories were modernized. The site of the former mens' toilet was converted into the upmarket Café de Piaf, a project that cost some £200,000 and required the removal of 100 tons of rubble. This restaurant, which opened in 1986 and featured live piano music, was similar to the large restaurant that had opened in the early 1920s following the station's redevelopment, in that it targeted theatre-goers as well as commuters.

In the summer of 1988, Mercury Communications unveiled their new telephone booth design on Waterloo's concourse. Twenty-six payphones were installed near Platform 11, with the Trade and Industry Secretary Lord Young making the first call from Waterloo (to the chairman of Cable and Wireless, Sir Eric Sharp, to congratulate him on the system).

The booth's design – described by Mercury as 'the Corinthian look' – was very much of its time: a

British Rail Class 432 (3004), Waterloo, October 1983.

modernist design featuring long curves and painted blue metal. However, the bold new look didn't prove too popular: *The Kensington Post* described the boxes as a 'neo-Gothic horror', whilst passing commuters, when asked, described them as 'ugly things that look like Dr Who's Tardis', and 'horrible and absolutely horrendous'.

The main event to take place at Waterloo in the 1980s was the station's role in the royal wedding of Charles and Diana on 29 July 1981. Following the widely televised ceremony at St Paul's Cathedral, the newly wed couple were driven to Waterloo where they boarded the royal train (975025 *Caroline*) for a journey to Romsey, where they embarked upon their honeymoon.

In the late 1990s, Waterloo began seeing privatized rail services, with Stagecoach being awarded the contract.

Some years later, on 26 May 2005, the final slam-door train from Waterloo, the 11.35am to Bournemouth, departed the station; this brought a very distinct era of commuting to an end.

CHAPTER 10

Waterloo International

Waterloo International – London's first gateway to the Channel Tunnel – marked an important chapter in the station's history, and harked back to an era when special boat trains made Waterloo an exciting place linked with nations abroad. In hindsight, therefore, it is somewhat surprising to consider that this additional terminal operated for just thirteen years.

A LONG-HELD DREAM

Despite the historically turbulent relationship between Britain and France, there had been numerous attempts over the years to connect the two nations via a tunnel beneath the English Channel (or *la Manche* if viewing it from a French perspective). Incredibly, the concept predated railway travel, the first suggestion having been made by mining engineer Albert Mathieu in 1802. Proposed during the Treaty of Amiens (which marked a brief lull in hostilities before the outbreak of the Napoleonic Wars), Mathieu envisioned an oil lamp-lit tunnel through which horse-drawn carriages could trot, pausing midway at an artificial island for rest.

The first idea for a railway beneath the Channel was put forward by another French engineer: Aimé Thomé de Gamond in the 1830s. Gamond was passionate about his vision, so much so that, with the help of his daughter, Elizabeth, he bravely collected geological samples from the Channel bed using a makeshift diving suit. Despite support for his proposal from both heads of state and fellow engineers – including Brunel and Robert Stephenson – Gamond died penniless.

Tunnelling attempts were undertaken in 1880 and 1974. Then in the late 1970s, a joint project between British Rail and France's SNCF was proposed – a rail link dubbed 'the Mousehole', a single-track tunnel through which convoys of up to ten trains would alternate in each direction. Based on a three-hour cycle, it was estimated this would allow for an efficient service to run.

Back In London

With the idea of a Channel tunnel taking shape, planners in London began considering sites where such a link could terminate. By early 1980, the Greater London Council (GLC), in discussion with British Rail, had drawn up a list of eight possibilities: London Bridge, Waterloo, Bricklayers Arms, Nine Elms, Olympia, West Brompton, Victoria and the Docklands – the latter three being preferred by the GLC. However, on 2 June 1981 *The Times* reported that 'Waterloo is emerging as the probable London terminal for a Channel tunnel'.

The reasons for this turnaround were that the road network around West Brompton was considered unsuitable; that Victoria, with its increasing ties to Gatwick Airport, was at risk of becoming saturated; and that the Docklands were 'not really taken seriously' – for it must be remembered that back then this area was an industrial wasteland, yet to undergo redevelopment. The same article went on to say:

Ways have been found to accommodate the tunnel traffic at Waterloo by bringing it up from the Kent coast towards Victoria as far as Battersea, then turning off to Waterloo where four new platforms could be built on the river side of the station.

Choose Your Crossing

In Britain, the government were supportive of a Channel crossing scheme, although adamant that it should be privately funded. In 1981, PM Margaret Thatcher and French president François Mitterrand agreed to examine the prospect of such an enterprise, and in April 1985, proposals were invited. This resulted in the following four schemes being shortlisted:

Eurobridge: A vast suspension bridge for cars, with the roads contained in an enclosed tube 70m (230ft) above the Channel. Estimated cost: £5.9 billion.

Euroroute: A road connected via a chain of tunnels and bridges, linked together by an artificial island. Estimated cost: £5 billion.

Channel Expressway: A tunnel shared by cars and trains. This scheme required ventilation shafts, which would have jutted up in the middle of the Channel. Estimated cost: £2.1 billion.

Eurotunnel: A straightforward railway tunnel. Estimated cost: £2.3 billion.

Although Thatcher favoured a road option, the risks associated with accidents and fumes were significant, thus making Eurotunnel the prime choice. Soon after, the Treaty of Canterbury and the Channel Tunnel Act were signed in 1986 and 1987 respectively, thus allowing the project to commence.

OPPOSITION TO WATERLOO INTERNATIONAL

In the Channel Tunnel Act it was made clear that the enterprise was private; any government investment was forbidden. As BR were still nationalized at the time, they therefore had to abandon their previous plans, although they backed Eurotunnel and were still able to commit to spending on related facilities, as this would prove beneficial to their own operations. With Waterloo earmarked as the main terminus, it was announced in January 1986 that BR planned to build four platforms (later five) at Waterloo, each being 400m (438yd) long and located to the north of those used by the Richmond, Reading and Windsor lines.

For some local residents, plans for an international terminal and the estimated 20 million extra passengers it would bring, caused considerable alarm. Their fears were supported by both the Bishop of Southwark, who believed the project would be 'the death knell for community life in the area', and the chairman of Lambeth's planning committee, Robert Colenutt, who claimed the development 'would transform the present character of the Waterloo area, and have serious adverse effects on the present community.'

In October 1986, a select committee was established to provide a forum for local groups. This was chaired by Alexander Fletcher, who was faced with 5,000 petitioners – although he conceded that '...five thousand petitions do not mean 5,000 issues.' Alert to residents' concerns, BR distributed 85,000 leaflets in January 1987 to households in Lambeth and Southwark to promote their cause, and a 'Channel Tunnel rail-link information centre' was opened at Waterloo itself.

Opposition was finally put to bed in May 1987 when a House of Lords select committee agreed that Waterloo should be the London terminus for Channel trains.

CONSTRUCTING WATERLOO INTERNATIONAL

Waterloo International's architectural contract was awarded to Sir Nicholas Grimshaw, whose firm worked in conjunction with Sir Alexander Gibb & Partners and Bovis. The building's long, undulating, stainless-steel roof containing 1,500 panes of glass was designed as a homage to the mighty railway engine sheds of the nineteenth century, although Grimshaw was quoted as saying that the building 'should last longer than the Victorians'.

The terminal's manner of construction emulated another nineteenth-century icon: the Crystal Palace, with its trusses being mass produced and assembled on site. Journalists at the time likened the new terminal to a 'high-tech python curling round the side of old Waterloo', and a 'steel armadillo'. In May 1993, *The Times* called it 'the most impressive station building project since the Victorian railway age'.

Naturally the terminal was designed to incorporate customs facilities, a lounge area and so on, just like an airport. A glass wall, through which Waterloo's Victory Arch entrance was visible, separated the two terminals. The platforms were numbered 20 to 24, replacing the original 20 and 21, which had been demolished. Grimshaw's £130 million design was completed in good time – a year before the Channel Tunnel itself was open.

The building won both the European Union Prize for Contemporary Architecture Award, and the Royal Institute of British Architects' Steel Structure Building of the Year. When awarding this latter prize, RIBA chairman Dr Francis Duffy said the terminal 'creates its own wholly convincing urban order amid inner-city squalor'.

A large site, tailor made for servicing the Class 373 Eurostar trains, was established at North Pole depot (named so after a nearby pub) close to Wormwood Scrubs, approximately 6 miles (10km) from Waterloo. Meanwhile, a simulator for training drivers in the handling of the new Eurostar trains was installed in Holmes House, on Holmes Terrace, a short street tucked beside Waterloo Station.

Official Opening of the Channel Tunnel

The Channel Tunnel was officially opened on 6 May 1994. On that day the Queen was accompanied by British Rail chairman Sir Bob Reid, who provided a tour of Waterloo's new terminal; after this a plaque was unveiled. For the event, a ten-minute long musical arrangement entitled 'Music for the

Waterloo International under construction, 1992.

*Eurostar at Waterloo
International, 2006.*

*Waterloo
International roof.*

Eurostar passing Battersea, October 1995.

Royal Eurostar' was composed by Paul Patterson. An art installation by Jean-Luc Vilmouth, featuring a shoal of fish swimming in the air, added further culture.

After the formalities, the Queen boarded a train at Platform 24, along with PM John Major, former PM Margaret Thatcher and other dignitaries. They travelled to Calais, where the Queen met with François Mitterrand for an official inauguration ceremony. The train used for this historic trip was driven by thirty-six-year-old Nigel Brown, who had already conducted several test runs.

However, it would not be until the autumn of 1994 that Waterloo International was finally opened to the public.

A Brief Flame

When Eurostar services ran from Waterloo they were painfully slow on the British side, trundling through south London on twisting Victorian lines via Stewarts Lane. It was only once on the French side that the modern, 'shark-like' 373s could finally hit their stride.

This was not the original intention, of course. When the route was being planned, there were ambitions to have far more efficient running via a tunnel dug beneath south London. This caused much controversy, however, due to the disruption – particularly around Peckham's Warwick Gardens area – that would have ensued.

It was also hoped that a second terminus – an underground complex designed by Sir Norman Foster and connected to Waterloo via another tunnel – would have been created, sandwiched between King's Cross and St Pancras. Although this link never materialized, St Pancras is now indeed home to London's Channel Tunnel terminal – and it had long been known that this was going to be the case.

As early as 1993 – before Waterloo International had even opened – moves had been made to eventually

Overlooking Waterloo International's former concourse.

transfer operations to St Pancras, where the proposed High Speed 1 line would provide a swifter route to the Channel. In this respect, therefore, Waterloo International mirrored Waterloo's early history when, back in the 1840s, the first terminal at Nine Elms had held the fort until it became feasible for the L&SWR to locate to a more practical location.

The last Eurostar to leave Waterloo International was an 18.12 service to Brussels, which departed on 3 November 2007.

WATERLOO INTERNATIONAL TODAY

After 2007 Waterloo International was mothballed, and as the years passed it became decidedly scruffy. In 2011, however, the platforms were given a new lease of life – as a theatre for staging a version of *The Railway Children*, complete with a fully working steam engine.

In 2018 the platforms were brought back into use for regular service following an £800 million refit. They are now a true asset to twenty-first century Waterloo: sharp, clean and modern, with Grimshaw's architecture restored to its former glory.

Waterloo International today.

A shopping mall is planned for the area beneath the former international terminal. Along with other developments – such as the removal of the Elizabeth House office block, which has obscured the view of Waterloo from York Road since the 1960s – this will ensure that the UK's largest railway terminal remains a major landmark for many decades to come.

Waterloo concourse, August 2020.

Waterloo in Culture

Since it has played a key role in London life for over 170 years, it is not surprising that Waterloo features in many examples of art, film and literature. The following are some notable appearances.

FILM AND TELEVISION

Bank Holiday (1938)

Directed by Carol Reed, *Bank Holiday* focuses on three couples catching trains to the seaside. The film features some wonderful on-location footage of 1930s Waterloo, including steam engines, a panorama of the packed concourse, and the busy Cab Road. Interestingly, it would appear that a number of scenes were shot on a set built to resemble the station as it appeared at the time, including a mock-up of Boots the chemist and Waterloo's News Cinema.

The Bourne Ultimatum (2007)

In an electrifying scene, journalist Simon Ross (played by Paddy Considine) is pursued across Waterloo's bustling concourse by CIA agents. Fortunately, he is aided by Jason Bourne (Matt Damon), and the pair work together to outwit their sinister pursuers.

Aerial view of trains at Waterloo.

The Good Die Young (1954)

Although the scene is brief, this crime thriller features some detailed views of Waterloo's concourse – including the large departure board and a booth for theatre tickets, topped by the Johnnie Walker whiskey mascot. A shot of the main Victory Arch entrance – then begrimed in 1950s soot – is also included.

Harry's Game (1982)

In the opening scene of this tense television series, IRA hitman Billy Downes (played by Derek Thompson) is seen leaving Waterloo en route to assassinate a cabinet minister.

Horror Hospital (1973)

This horror film starring Robin Askwith features Waterloo early on. Good views of the old, wooden departure board can be seen, as can the cinema – which by this point had closed for good.

Jhoom Barabar Jhoom (2007)

In the opening credits to this romantic comedy, Amitabh Bachchan – widely regarded to be India's most famous actor – leads a large crowd in a lavish Bollywood dance on Waterloo's concourse.

Just Another Day (1983)

In a way, *Just Another Day* can be viewed as the spiritual successor to *Terminus* (*see* below). Filmed by John Pitman, this documentary provides a marvellous insight into Waterloo as it was during the early 1980s, with a special focus on the staff who keep the terminal running.

London Terminus (1944)

This fifteen-minute film provides a vivid account of a day in the life of Waterloo during World War II. The station concourse, signal box, news cinema and the arches beneath the terminal – then a hive of activity – can all be seen.

Miss London Ltd (1943)

The opening of this musical comedy depicts Waterloo during wartime, and includes a good view of the News Cinema. The musical number to which the scene plays includes the catchy line 'The 8.50 choo-choo to Waterloo choo-choos in on platform 13'!

On the Beat (1962)

In this Norman Wisdom film, Norman Pitkin is desperate to follow in his father's footsteps by becoming a Metropolitan Police Officer. At the beginning of the film, Norman attempts a citizen's arrest on the Bank end of the Waterloo & City line (featuring 1940 stock carriages) – with alarming results.

Only Fools and Horses (1988)

Broadcast on Christmas Day 1988, the *Only Fools and Horses* episode *Dates* features Waterloo as the place where Derek Trotter first meets his future love interest, Raquel Turner. The pair meet beneath Waterloo's clock, and as they walk off, Derek confuses *Brief Encounter* with *Close Encounters of the Third Kind*!

Ooh You are Awful (1972)

In this feature-length Dick Emery film we are treated to an inside view of the former station announcer's box – which of course provides excellent views across the station. What Emery gets up to next, however – involving a photo booth on Waterloo's concourse – probably wouldn't get made today.

The Party's Over (1965)

When it was first released in 1965 this film, starring Oliver Reed, proved controversial. Some good views of Waterloo's platforms can be seen towards the end of the film, in which a coffin is loaded on to an awaiting train.

The Pot Carriers (1962)

The opening to prison drama, *The Pot Carriers* has an aerial view of Waterloo, complete with steam locomotives. There are also views of an electric suburban service on Platform 1, and a view from the Victory Arch, looking towards Cab Road.

Return of a Stranger (1937)

A drama film in which views of steam engines at Waterloo, along with cabs waiting inside the station, can be seen.

Return to Waterloo (1984)

Directed by The Kinks' Ray Davies, *Return to Waterloo* is a disturbing musical, set on board a commuter train making its way from Guildford to Waterloo. An album of the same name was released to coincide with the project.

Ring of Spies (1964)

Ring of Spies tells the true story of the Portland Spy Ring, which passed top secret naval intelligence to the Soviets before being uncovered in 1961. Two of the ring's members, Harry Houghton and Ethel Gee, were arrested after they arranged a rendezvous at Waterloo. Gee was found to be carrying a shopping bag, inside which was a large amount of classified material – including details on Britain's first nuclear submarine, the HMS *Dreadnought*.

The film replicates their meeting and arrest, and as such features Waterloo station, including the station approach road and several other surrounding streets.

Rush Hour (1970)

Made by British Transport Films, *Rush Hour* is a fun short in which time-lapse photography depicts the many trains and thousands of commuters passing through Waterloo.

Seven Days to Noon (1950)

In this thriller, a scientist steals an atomic warhead and threatens to detonate it in the capital. Waterloo appears several times: at the beginning of the film before the crisis starts, and then later on, when the station is used to evacuate Londoners. Waterloo's left luggage office also makes an appearance.

Sliding Doors (1998)

Starring Gwyneth Paltrow as main protagonist Helen, *Sliding Doors* presents two alternating story lines, which split at a key moment: in one, Helen manages to board a tube train; in the second she misses it. This plot device was filmed at the Waterloo end of the Waterloo & City line.

Survivors (1976)

Series Two of this post-apocalyptic drama features a two-part story entitled *Lights of London*, in which a small community is discovered in the remains of the capital. Part Two features a shoot-out on the Bank End of the Waterloo & City line – which, for the purposes of the story, is made to look like Oval Station.

The Sweeney (1976)

The concourse at Waterloo can be seen briefly in the episode *Selected Target*, when a recently released prisoner makes his way to London. The scene is interesting because it is possible to hear the music that was played over the station's tannoy system at the time (*see* also *Just Another Day*, detailed above).

Taxi! (1963)

This early 1960s comedy starred Sid James, who, as the show's title suggests, played a London cabbie. In an episode titled *The Runaway Girl* Waterloo featured as a location – but sadly the episode is long lost.

Terminus (1961)

Terminus is, quite simply, a masterpiece, and by far the definitive portrayal of Waterloo on film. Directed

Images from Terminus, *1961.*

by John Schlesinger, it features one day in the life of Waterloo, filmed in a 'fly-on-the-wall' style with no commentary and an evocative jazz soundtrack.

Amongst the scenes portrayed are the rush hour, the station's telephone exchange, the station announcer's box, the signal box (complete with resident cat), Windrush generation arrivals (*see* Chapter 9) and a party of prisoners (who were in fact played by actors, although prisoner transfer by railway was indeed common at the time) being escorted on to a train.

Perhaps most famous, though, is young Matthew Perry, who sobs his heart out when he realizes he's lost his mother. Matthew's tears are real – Schlesinger manufactured a scenario in which the youngster was made to believe he really was abandoned!

Terminus has been made public domain, and can be found online.

Terminus (1955)

Not to be confused with the 1961 short film (*see* above), this *Terminus* was a television series written by Phillip Odell, who said:

> *I have based the series on the little game most people play when travelling – wondering who the stranger is sitting opposite, where he is going and for what reason.*

With each story starting at Waterloo, this series made its debut on Saturday 27 May 1955 with an episode entitled *Margin for Error* starring Ursula Howells and André Morell. Sadly this television series is now long lost.

Underground (1928)

This silent classic features a scene filmed, as the title suggests, on Waterloo's tube section, primarily around the busy escalators.

The Waterloo Bridge Handicap (1978)

This comedy short, starring Leonard Rossiter (*see* also *The Death of Reginald Perrin*), Lynda Bellingham and Gordon Kaye depicts a group of commuters heading into Waterloo from Surbiton on a morning rush-hour train. Once at Waterloo, the race is on to see who can exit the terminal and cross Waterloo Bridge the fastest – and all set to a horse-race style commentary!

Waterloo Road (1945)

In this film Jim Colter (played by John Mills) deserts from the army in order to save his wife from a conscription dodger named Ted Purvis. The film features some wonderful views of Waterloo, including the concourse, platforms, and both steam and electric trains.

The Wrecker (1929)

The unusual premise of this silent film is that a villain deliberately sets out to cause train crashes. Both Waterloo's concourse and the (then very new) Victory Arch can be seen, along with a scene shot on a platform.

ART

Terence Cuneo (1907–1996)

In 1967, artist Terence Cuneo was commissioned by the Science Museum to paint the concourse at Waterloo for display at their new Land Transport gallery. The resulting piece was huge, measuring 20 by 10ft (6 by 3m), and is packed with detail. The artwork is now on display at The National Railway Museum, York.

Statue of Terence Cuneo at Waterloo, 2014.

Between 2004 and 2014, a statue of Terence Cuneo was on display outside Waterloo's former Eurostar terminal. It can now be found at Brompton Barracks in Kent, home of the Corps of Royal Engineers, with whom Cuneo served in World War II.

Feliks Topolski (1907–1989)

In 1975, Polish-born artist Feliks Topolski opened a studio close to Waterloo; it was based on Concert Hall Approach, within an arch on the line between Waterloo East and Charing Cross. Here he created his *Memoir of a Century*, a 600ft (183m) long mural depicting events from the twentieth century. Officially unveiled in 1984, the paintings remain in place today.

Helen McKie (1889–1957)

During World War II, artist Helen McKie created a series of illustrations documenting wartime activity at Waterloo. These intriguing sketches feature female railway workers, shops and kiosks, an escalator carrying service personnel, and even the entrance to Waterloo's cinema – complete with a Mickey Mouse and Donald Duck advertising display.

Topolski Gallery.

Leake Street graffiti tunnel.

More famously, McKie was commissioned to create two wonderful views of Waterloo – showing the terminal in peace and war – to celebrate the station's 100th anniversary.

Leake Street Arches

In recent years, Leake Street has become known as the 'Graffiti Tunnel': a long space where budding artists are permitted to spray designs and murals. The results are something to behold, and as the designs change frequently, repeat visits are always rewarded.

William Blake Murals

Poet and artist William Blake (1742–1814) once lived on Hercules Road, long before the railway arrived. For this reason, a number of murals inspired by his work may be discovered in the streets and arches surrounding Waterloo.

LITERATURE

The Death of Reginald Perrin (1975)

In David Nobbs' novel, weary commuter Reginald Perrin – a middle-aged, middle manager for Sunshine Deserts – commutes into Waterloo every day, and every day his train is exactly eleven minutes late. For this irregularity, British Rail come up with a different excuse each time, ranging from staff difficulties at Hampton Wick to 'reaction to rolling stock shortages at Nine Elms'. This absurdity is one of the many

William Blake mural, Carlisle Lane.

The Lonely Londoners (1956)

The opening to this novel by Sam Selvon is set at Waterloo station (*see* Chapter 9).

The Necropolis Railway (2005)

Set in 1903, this novel by Andrew Martin uses the Necropolis railway as the background to a detective story.

Sherlock Holmes: The Adventure of the Speckled Band (1892)

In this short story, Holmes and Watson head to Waterloo to catch a train to Surrey. Before setting off, Holmes asks Watson to make sure he takes a revolver.

Three Men in a Boat (1889)

This classic tale by Jerome K. Jerome famously features a description of the old Waterloo, summarizing how confusing the layout was during the nineteenth century (*see* Chapter 3).

War of the Worlds (1898)

Waterloo is mentioned several times in H.G. Wells' early science fiction classic, including a scene in which a troop train passes through the terminal (*see* Chapter 5).

The Wrong Box (1889)

Co-written by Robert Louis Stevenson and Lloyd Osbourne, *The Wrong Box* tells the story of two brothers who are the last surviving members of a tontine: in others words, whoever lives the longest will inherit a fortune. Waterloo is mentioned numerous times in the novel, including a scene in which a cab driver is urged to hurry to 'Waterloo Station for your life. Sixpence for yourself!'

frustrations in Reggie's life, which eventually lead him to fake his own death.

Reggie does have fond memories of Waterloo though: long ago, it was there, on a station bench, that he had his first kiss with his wife, Elizabeth.

The novel was famously adapted by the BBC in 1976, as a sitcom entitled *The Fall and Rise of Reginald Perrin*, with Leonard Rossiter turning Reggie into one of his most iconic roles.

London Belongs to Me (1945)

Norman Collins' 1945 classic depicts 1930s and 1940s London in wonderful detail. Waterloo appears when, following the outbreak of war, children are evacuated from the station (*see* Chapter 8).

MUSIC

'Smithers Jones' (1979)

In this song by The Jam, Smithers Jones is a pin-stripe-suited commuter who catches the train into Waterloo every morning. Unlike Reginald Perrin (*see* above), Smithers Jones seems to enjoy his work life – so it's rather tragic when he's called into the office to be let go.

'Vindaloo' (1998)

Released by 'Fat Les' (aka Keith Allen) to coincide with the 1998 World Cup, this football song contains the lyric:

> *Me and me Mum and me Dad and me Gran*
> *We're off to Waterloo*
> *Me and me Mum and me Dad and me Gran*
> *And a bucket of Vindaloo*

The World Cup that year took place in France, meaning the lyric is a reference to the Eurostar, which at the time, ran from Waterloo.

'Waterloo Sunset' (1967)

Easily the popular song most associated with Waterloo, 'Waterloo Sunset' was released in 1967 (coincidentally, the same year in which steam locomotives ceased operating from the station). As well as mentioning the 'millions of people swarming like flies round Waterloo Underground', we're also told about Terry and Julie, who meet at 'Waterloo Station every Friday night…'.

'West End Girls' (1985)

In the music video for this classic Pet Shop Boys single, Neil Tennant and Chris Lowe stride across Waterloo's concourse.

Waterloo station, 1984.

Bibliography

www.british-history.ac.uk

Chapman, Frederick and Marshall, Dendy *A History of the Southern Railway* (The Curwen Press, 1936).

Cherry, Bridget and Pevsner, Nikolaus *The Buildings of England, London 2: South* (Yale University Press, 1983).

Chivers, Colin and Wood, Philip *Waterloo Station circa 1900: An illustrated tour* (The South Western Circle, 2006).

Christopher, John *Waterloo Station Through Time* (Amberley Publishing, 2013).

www.davidrumsey.com

www.distantwriting.co.uk

Fareham, John *The History of Waterloo Station* (Bretwalda Books, 2013).

Fay, Sam *A Royal Road: Being the History of the South Western Railway, from 1825 to the present* (1882).

Freeling, Arthur *The London and Southampton Railway Companion: Containing a Complete Description of Everything Worthy of Attention on the Line* (J.T. Norris, 1839).

Gordon, William John *Our Home Railways, How they began and how they are worked* (Frederick Warne, 1910).

www.gracesguide.co.uk

Marsden, Colin J *This is Waterloo* (Ian Allan Ltd, 1981).

The Oxford Dictionary of National Biography www.oxforddnb.com

Railway Wonders of the World, Volume 1: The Story of the Southern (Amalgamated Press, 1935).

Smiles, Samuel *The Life of George Stephenson, Railway Engineer* (John Murray, 1874).

The Southern Counties Railway Society.

Wakeford, Iain *Woking 150: The History of Woking and its Railway* (Mayford and Woking District History Society, 1987).

Wyld, James *The South Western, or London, Southampton and Portsmouth Railway Guide* (James Wyld, 1839).

Illustration Credits

Index

ABBA 138
Abney Park Cemetery 53
accidents
    construction 19, 106
    horse-drawn 43–44
    Necropolis Station 67
    Nine Elms 19
    Waterloo & City Railway 92
    Waterloo East 80–81
Acton Depot 44, 96
Addington Street 101
Agate, James 7, 122
air-raids
    shelter 39, 124, 129
    siren 139
    World War I 112
    World War II 126–127
airlock 89, 90
Alaska Street 73
Albert Memorial 117
Aldershot 104
Aldwych 127
Alfie 31
All Saints Church 102
Allen, Keith 155
Aloetta, Moses 153
Altenburg Gardens 117
American Car Foundry Company 97
American Embassy 12
Andrews, Catherine 19
Anglicans 57
Antwerp 90
Archbishop's Park 102
arches
    area beneath Waterloo 113, 124
    coffin storage 56
    construction 28
    Leake Street 153
    Miles Street 28
    Minories 26
    Necropolis Railway 58
    on marshy terrain 30
    removal of 106
    substructure 46
    support 34
    Tinworth Street 29
    viaduct 25
    widening 39
    World War II 150
Armistice 114
Askwith, Robin 150
Astley's Amphitheatre 98
Aston, Ron 138
Athena, goddess 118
Attercliffe 11
Aubin Street 46, 94, 100, 102
Auxiliary Air Force 125

Bachchan, Amitabh 150
Bain, Alexander 19
Baird, John Logie 122
Baker Street & Waterloo Railway Act 96
Bakerloo line 96–97, 124, 126
Ballard, Annie Louisa 114
Bank

Junction 82, 87, 90
    Station 91, 94, 150, 151
    Travolator 95–96
Bank Holiday 149
Battersea 12, 22, 75, 97, 106, 117, 143, 146
Battersea Wharf 38
Baylis Road 95
Baylis, Lillian 112
Bazalgette, Joseph 85
Beluga whale 45
Belvedere Road 49, 85, 101, 130, 134
Bridegroom steamboat 19
British European Airways (BEA) 131, 132
British Expeditionary Force 125
British News Theatres Ltd 121
British Rail
    British Rail Blue 94
    chairman of 144
    Class 373 Eurostar 145, 146
    Class 411 81
    Class 487 94, 95, 96
    logo 96
    The Death of Reginald Perrin 153
British Railways 127, 130, 137
British Transport Films 151
British Transport Police 39, 134
Brixton 134
Brompton Barracks 153
Brookwood
    bars 58, 68
    coffin ticket 59
    consecration 57
    fencing 57
    line closure 68
    military cemetery 68
    North Cemetery Station 57, 69
    Railway Avenue 57
    road transport 68
    South Cemetery Station 57, 59
    tracks 61, 69
Broun, Richard 54
Brown, Nigel 146
Browne, Francis 108
Brunel, Isambard Kingdom 72, 142
Brunswick House 14
Brunswick Yard 38
Brush Company 49
Brush, Charles Francis 49
Brussels 147
Buckingham Palace 114
Bugle Hall 9
Bull Ring 140

Cab Road 121, 130, 137, 149
Cabmen's Shelter Fund 43
cabs 15, 20, 21, 129
Cafe de Piaf 140
Calais 146

California 155
Cambridge University 112
Cambridge, Duke of 92
camouflage 124
Campbell Buildings 102
Canada 108, 123, 125
canals 8–9, 10
Cannon Street 73, 75, 78, 88, 89, 94, 134
Canova, Antonio 31
Cardboard City 139–140
Caribbean 133
Carlisle 16
carriages *see* Rolling Stock
Carrick, Earl of 112
Casey Jones Burger Bar 140
Central Station 45, 46, 94, 108
Chamberlain, Neville 126
Channel Crossing Scheme 143
Channel Expressway 143
Chaplin, Charlie 117, 153
Charing Cross 24, 76, 77, 78, 80, 81, 96, 126, 153
Charing Cross Bridge 81, 84
Charing Cross Railway Company 72, 75
Charing Cross roof collapse 106
Charing Cross, Euston & Hampstead Railway 97
Chartley Place 102
Chatham & Dover Railway 87
Chelsea Pensioner 68
Cheltenham 117
Chertsey 36
Chessington Zoo 137
Chichele Road 113
Chiswick 16
Christies Place 102
Churchill, Winston 69, 134–135
Citizen steamboat 21
City & South London Railway 88, 97
City for the Dead 54
City of London & Richmond Railway 21, 22
Clapham Common station 17
Clapham Junction 17, 22, 23, 42, 63, 105
Clapham Rail Disaster 17
Clapham Road 139
Clerkenwell 53
Clifton Suspension Bridge 72
Coade Stone Lion 129–130
Coade, Eleanor 129
coffin lift 58, 61
Colenutt, Robert 143
collection dogs 106
College Wharf 84
Collins, Norman 154
Colney Hatch 66
commuter belt 17, 21
compressed air 90
concourse at Waterloo
    clock above 7, 118
    early 20th century 110, 120, 121
    Eurostar 147

film & television appearances 149, 150, 151, 152, 155
    in the 19th Century 45
    loudspeaker 123, 125
    music played on 123, 151
    public relations events 137
    rolling stock on display 114–115
    telephone kiosks 140
    track across 49, 73–75, 77, 78, 80
    World War II 123, 124
Coney Island 45
Considine, Paddy 149
Cooke, Alistair 124
Cooke, William Fothergill 18
Corfu, RMS 129
Cornhill 90
Cornwall Road 89, 100, 109
Cornwall, Sir Edwin 97
Corps of Royal Engineers 153
Corpse station 58
Cosser Street 127
Cournet, Frederic 37
Covent Garden 43, 101
Crane, Waterloo & City line 95
Crewe 62
Cricklewood 113
Crimewatch 139
Cross Bones Graveyard 53
Cross Street 45
Crystal Palace 36, 38, 144
Crystal Palace Park 83
Crystal Palace Pneumatic Railway 83
Cuba 124
Cubitt, Lewis 71
Cubitt, William 55
Cuneo, Terrence 152
Cunliff, Mitzi 130
Cuper's Pleasure Gardens 129
cut and cover tunnel 82–83
Cut, The 87
Cyprus station 50

D-Day 127
Dagenham Marshes 90
Damon, Matt 149
Dardanelles 118
Davies, Ray 151
Davis, Alexander 106
Davis, H.G 129
Death of Reginald Perrin 152
Delaware 91
Derby Day 17, 36
deserter 114
Dick Kerr Works 94
Direct Messenger Company 105
Directomat 135
Ditton Marsh 12, 17, 21
Docklands 142, 143
Docklands Light Railway 90
Dome of Discovery 130
Dottin, Abel Rous 9
Douglas, Lord 152
Dover 73, 75, 80
Dover Castle Hotel 66
Dover Strait 8

Dr Who 141
'Drain' 96
Dreadnought, HMS 151
driver training 144
Drummond locomotive 61
Drury Lane 61
Duck, Donald 153
Duddy, John 29
Duffy, Dr Francis 144
Duke Street 89
Dunkirk 125
Durnsford Road 92, 116

Eardley sidings 94
Earls Court 152
Early of Onslow 54
Earth to Earth coffin 60
East Counties Railway
    Company 72
Eastcheap 134
Edwards, 'Buster' 139
Egypt 118
Elder Dempster Lines 135
electric indicators 47
electric lighting 49, 90
electric telegraph 18
Electric Tramway Company of
    Preston 94
Elephant sculpture 98
Elizabeth House 130, 148
Elmers End 80
embezzlement 78
Emery, Dick 150
Emmett, John Thomas 23
Epsom Racecourse 17
Eros 56
escalator 94, 152, 153
Eurobridge 143
Euroroute 143
Eurotunnel 143
Euston station 18, 68, 75, 76,
    85, 97
evacuation 126
Ewer Street 57
Exeter 16, 42

Falconbridge 22, 25, 42
Fall & Rise of Reginald Perrin
    154
Farmer, Frederick 92
Farnborough 78
Farringdon 82
Fentiman Road 117
Ferdinand, Archduke 110
Festival Hall Pier 134
Festival of Britain 130–131
Fletcher, Alexander 143
Fletcher, Ken 139
floodgates 126
flooding 139
Fontaine, Joan 122
Footbridge 47, 72, 81, 138
Ford, David 67
Ford, Lieutenant Colonel 101
Foster, Sir Norman 146
France 118, 124
Frances Street 81
Fulwell 51

Galbraith, William 89
Gammond, Aime Thome de
    142
Garman, Arthur 113

gas masks 125
Gatwick 94, 143
Gee, Ethel 151
General Post Office 44, 83, 120
Gents of Leicester 118
Giles, Francis 10, 11
giraffe 45
Glasgow 69
glass roof 68, 124, 131
Goldsmid, Sir Francis 48, 49
Good Die Young, The 150
Gosport 18
Gotha Bomber 114
graffiti tunnel 153
Granby Place 100, 102
Grand Junction Railway 11
Granger, Milford 114
Grassemann, C 129
Graves, Robert 112
Great Depression, The 31, 81
Great Exhibition, The 36, 38
Great Northern London
    Cemetery Company 68
Great St Thomas Apostle Street
    87
'Great Stink' 37
Great Train Robbery, The 139
'Great Transformation' 99
Great Western, SS 18
Great Western Railway 10, 18
Greater London Council 142
Greathead Shield 88, 89, 90
Greathead, James Henry 88,
    89, 90, 91, 96
Greet Street 139
Grenadier Guards 125
Griffin Street 44, 100, 101,
    102, 129
Grimshaw, Sir Nicholas 144, 147
Guildford 8, 24, 25, 47, 151
Guildford Junction Railway 24

haggis 137
Hampton Court 19, 36, 47, 50,
    114, 116
Hampton Wick 153
Harlesden 75
Harlesden Green 22
Harry's Game 150
Haste, Kendra 98
Hatton Garden 49
Hawes, R.D 105
Hayley, Bill 133
Hayworth, Rita 133
Heathrow 151
helicopter station 132
Henry, Leonard 123
Hercules Road 102
Heron, John 139
Hersham Green 12
Hibbert, John 38
High Speed One 147
Highgate Cemetery 53
Hills, Graham Arthur 138
Hitchock, Alfred 122
holidaymakers 128
Holland 124
Holmes House 144
Holmes Terrace 102, 144
Holmes, Sherlock 154
Hood, Jacomb J.W. 46, 105, 110
Hop Exchange 87
Hornet locomotive 32

Horns Tavern 25, 26
Horror Hospital 150
horses
    acquirement of 38
    Brookwood Cemetery 57
    conveying rolling stock 97
    funeral service 56
    horse-drawn carriage 142
    Impulsoria experimental
        locomotive 35
    Waterloo Bridge Handicap
        152
    Waterloo Junction 77
    working conditions 33, 41,
        43–44, 52, 107
    World War I 112
Houghton, Harry 151
Hounslow loop 42, 116
House of Lords 100, 102, 143
Howell, York 70
Howells, Ursula 152
Hugo, Victor 37
Hungerford Bridge 22, 25, 35,
    71, 72, 81, 132
Hungerford Market 24, 26, 72
'Hut', the 113

IMAX cinema 140
Imperial College 104
Impulsoria, the 35
Indian Army 114
Industrial Revolution 53
Irish Guards 125
Irish Republican Army 135,
    150
Irish, Edward 68
Isle of Dogs 84
Isle of Wight Steam Railway
    135

Jackson & Sharp Company 91
Jam, The 154
James, Robert 27
James, Sid 151
Japan 129
Jerome, Jerome K. 50, 154
Jhoom Barabar Jhoom 150
John Mowlem & Co 89
John Street 73
Johnston, Robert 9
Jubilee Gardens 84
Jubilee line 95, 96, 98
Just Another Day 150

Kaye, Gordon 152
Keaton, Buster 133
Kempton Racecourse 11
Kennington 25, 102
Kennington Green 100
Kennington Road 60, 97
Kensal Green Cemetery 53
Kensington 75
Kensington Air Station 131
Kent 153
Kenward, Reverend 114
Kew 116
Kew Bridge 16
Khartoum station 49
Kind Edward I 104
King Charles I statue 86
King Edward VII 106
King George V 118
King George VI 130

King George's Hospital 111
King Leopold 90
King William IV 93
King William Street 88
Kings Cross station 66, 146
Kingston 15, 17, 20, 21, 116, 47
Kinks, The 151
Knapp, Jimmy 69
Kunz, Charlie 133

Lambeth
    Borough Council 102
    Lambeth Coroners
        Court 81
    Lambeth Council 132
    Lambeth Marsh 129
    Lambeth North station
        97, 139
    Lambeth Palace 30
    Lambeth residents 29
    Lambeth Road 29
    Lambeth Vestry 100,
        101, 102
    Lambeth, viaduct
        through 87
Lancashire 11
Lancaster Place 58, 60
Land Transport Gallery 152
Launcelot Street 92, 101
Leake Street 27, 47, 55, 58,
    102, 153
Leake, John 27
Leatherhead 47
Liberace 133
Lights of London 151
Lion Brewery 130
Little York Street 102
Liverpool & Manchester
    Railway 9, 10, 11
Liverpool Street station 89
Locke, Joseph 11, 19, 23, 24,
    27, 30
London & Birmingham
    Railway 18
London & Blackwell Railway
    18, 26
London & Brighton South Coast
    Railway 38
London & Greenwich Railway
    24, 26, 28, 71
London & North Western
    Railway 75
London Airport 131
London Belongs to Me 126, 154
London Bridge 37, 88, 93
London Bridge station 26, 36,
    27, 35, 71, 72, 73, 75, 76,
    87, 142
London clay 131
London County Council 81, 91,
    97, 100, 101, 102
London Jack 106
London National Guard 113
London Necropolis & National
    Mausoleum Company 54
London Tavern, The 9, 11
London Terminus 150
London Transport Museum 96
London Zoo 45
London, Brighton & South
    Coast Railway 75
London, Square Mile 7, 27, 37,
    76, 82, 88

Lonely Londoners, The 154
Loop line 42
Lord Shaftesbury 55, 56, 67
Lowe, Chris 155
Lower Marsh 100, 102, 105, 106, 107, 135, 139
luggage lift 47, 95
lying-in-hospital 27

MacDonald, Alistair 121
MacDonald, James Ramsay 121
Mackie, Gordon 138
mail train 19
Major, John 146
Mansion House 89, 90
Manx Tourist Board 137
Marble Hall Buffet 117
Martin, Andrew 142
Maudslay, Sons & Field 102
McKie, Helen 129, 153
Memoir of a Century 153
Merchant Navy Class locomotive 135, 136
Mesopotamia 118
Metropolitan Board of Works 43, 45, 85
Metropolitan District Railway 84
Metropolitan Extension Act 27
Metropolitan Railway 83, 96
Metropolitan Railway Commission 27
miasma 56
Miles Street 28
Millbank Penitentiary 14
Mills, Sir John 152
Ministry of Supply 125
Minories 26
Miss London Ltd 150
Mitterand, Francois 143
Morell, Andre 152
Morpeth Place 100
Mortlake 22
Mortlake station 23
Morton Place 127
Mountbatten, Lord 69, 135
Mouse, Mickey 121, 153
'Mousehole', the 142
murder
    Heron, John 139
    Hills, Graham Arthur 138
    O'Neil, Frank 139
    Soan, Josun 139
Muswell Hill 45

Napoleon 8
Napoleon III 78
Napoleonic Wars 8, 26, 142
National Gallery 27
National Liberal Club 97
National Provincial & Union Bank 120
National Railway Museum 92, 135, 152
National Rifle Association 41
Natural History Museum 117
navvies 19, 89
Nelson Square 87
Netherlands 125
Network South East 94, 98
New Southgate Crematorium 66

New York City 18, 45, 127
New Zealand
    Southland Railway 24
    troops 125
    Wellington Harbour 31
Newcastle-upon-Tyne 47
Newgate Gaol 37
Newington Butts 85
Newnham Terrace 100
News Theatre 121
newscaster 135
Nike, goddess 118
Nine Elms
    description of 13, 14
    distance from central London 71
    early terminal 11, 12, 15, 16, 17, 23, 70, 147
    extension from 20, 21, 22, 24, 25, 27, 28, 29, 31, 38
    locomotive works 32, 35, 62, 135, 153
    Necropolis railway 56
    Northern line station 97
    potential Eurotunnel site 142
    telegraph system 19
Nobbs, David 153
non-conformists 57
North Pole Depot 144
North Sea 118
North station 42, 49, 108
North, Edward Ford 66
Northern line 96, 97, 126
Northern line extension 97
Northolt 131
Northumberland House 26–27
Northumberland, Duke of 26
nuclear attack 139

O'Neil, Frank 139
Odell, Phillip 152
Old Kent Road 71
Old Vic Theatre 112
Olympia 142
Olympia Exhibition Hall 122
Omnibus
    Nine Elms 15, 19, 20
    Richmond 22
    Waterloo 32, 43, 44
On the Beat 150
Only Fools & Horses 150
Ooh You are Awful 150
Operation Diaper 129
Osbourne, Lloyd 154
Oval station 151
Overend, Gurney & Co Bank 85

Pacific, war in 128
Paddington 82
Pages Walk 71
Palestra Building 76
Pallingham 8
Paltrow, Gwyneth 151
Pan-Am 137
Panda Crossing 135
Parfett, Ned 108
Paris Metro fire 94
Parliament 11, 19, 22, 23, 24, 27, 38, 43, 53, 55, 56, 57, 71, 84, 87, 88, 91, 96, 100, 101, 131, 132

Party's Over, The 150
Pathe News 118
Patterson, Paul 146
Peckham 146
pedestrian subway 127
Pepys, Samuel 72
Percy, George 27
Percy, Hugh 26, 27
Perrin, Reginald 152, 153, 154, 155
Perry, Matthew 152
Pet Shop Boys 155
photo booth 150
Piccadilly Circus 56, 135
Pickfords 56
pinch wire 94
Pitman, John 150
Plymouth 104
pneumatic railway 83
porters 43, 45, 48, 50, 51, 52, 115
Portland Spy Ring 151
Portsea Island 8
Portsmouth 8, 9, 18, 104
Portsmouth & Arundel Canal 8
Post Office despatch tube 83
Pot Carriers, The 150
power station 92
Prince Charles 141
Princes Street 89
Princip, Gavrilo 110
privatization 141
Profumo, John 132
Prosser, William 24
Prussia, Prince & Princess of 73
Putney 22
Putney station 23

Queen Alexandra 106
Queen Elizabeth II 144
Queen Mary of Teck 118
Queen Street 87
Queen Victoria 12, 62, 73, 78, 93
Queen Victoria's private staton 35

Railway Children, The 147
Railway Pier 15
Railways Act 120
Reading 48
Reading station 42
Redcross Way 53
Reed, Oliver 150
refugees
    Belgian 114, 125
    Jewish 124
Regent Street 120
Reid, Sir Bob 144
Rennie, John 10
Return to Waterloo 151
Richmond 21, 22, 23, 25, 42, 51, 116, 143
Richmond & West End Junction Railway 22–23
Ring of Spies 151
River Thames 8, 12, 13, 14, 22, 24, 27, 37, 42, 72, 75, 81, 83, 84, 86, 87, 88, 89, 109, 132
River Wandle 23
River Wey 11
Roaring Twenties 120

Roberts, Harry 29
rolling stock
    accidents 19, 34, 48, 80, 81
    adaptation to electric traction 116
    complaints about 52
    early carriages 11, 12, 25, 42
    electric lighting in 49
    first to enter Waterloo 32
    Necropolis Railway 52, 62, 66, 68
    Nine Elms works 35
    on display at Waterloo 115
    overcrowding in 20, 36, 41, 128
    pneumatic carriage 83
    Titanic Special 108
    Waterloo & City Railway 91, 92, 93, 94, 95, 150
    Waterloo East 78
    World War I 114, 115
Rookwood Cemetery, Sydney 66
Root Bodied Forth sculpture 130
Rossiter, Leonard 152, 154
Rowland Hill's Chapel 76
Royal Engineers 30
Royal Exchange 16
Royal Festival Hall 130
Royal Institute of British Architects 144
Royal Mail 44
Royal Philharmonic Orchestra, Liverpool 158
Royal Train 141
Royal Wedding 141
Royal Windsor Steam Express 137
Rufford Street 66
Rush Hour 151
Russell, William George Mark 114

Salvation Army 112
Sandell Street 73, 79
Savoy Hotel 108
Schlesinger, John 152
Science Museum 152
Scotland Yard 84
Scottish Tourist Board 137
Secker Street 104
Seeds, Angela 139
Seven Days to Noon 151
Sevlon, Sam 133, 154
Shedden, Robert Jr 9
Shell Max House 124
Shell Tower 86, 152
Shepperton 47, 116
Siemens Brothers & Co. 92
Siemens, Sir Wilhelm 86
Siemens, Werner Von 86
signal box
    A Cabin 47, 61, 62
    Crow's Nest 54
    Terminus 152
Simmonds, Captain 30, 31
ski slope 137
Skylon 130
slam door train 141
Sliding Doors 151
Smithers Jones 154

Smithfield Market 89
Snake locomotive 32
SNCF 142
Soan, Josun 139
Society for Women's
    Suffrage 114
soda fountain 116
Solent 18
Somerset House 26
Somme, Battle of 112
South station 45, 46, 47, 49, 50,
    51, 108
South Western & City Junction
    Railway 87
South Western Railway Capital
    & Works Act 38
Southbank 134
Southampton
    Docks 18, 21, 36, 44,
        129, 133
    French arrivals 116
    London & Southampton
        Railway Company
        9, 10
    Services to and from
        Waterloo 22, 32, 42,
        52, 73, 104, 135
    Station 15, 16, 45
Southwark 55, 57, 87
Southwark & Hammersmith
    Railway 22
Southwark Bridge 22, 87
Southwark Underground
    station 76
Spa Fields burial ground 53
Spencer, Lady Diana 141
Speckled Band, The 154
Spry, Richard 54
St Anne's Church 61
St Anne's Parish 102
St George's Wharf 38
St John's Church 102
St Louis Ship 124
St Martin-in-the-Fields 61
St Pancras church 61
St Pancras Station 146
St Saviour's 57
St Saviour's Board of Works 87
St Thomas's Hospital 48, 92
Stagecoach Company 141
Stamford Street 89, 111
station announcer's box
    150, 151
station approach 43
stationmaster 51, 116
Stephenson, George 10, 11, 18
Stephenson, Robert 142
Stevenson, Robert Louis 154
Stewarts Lane 29, 146
Stockton & Darlington
    Railway 9

Stockton-on-Tees 89
Stockwell 88
Stovin, Cornelius 35
Strand Bridge 31
Strand, The 134
Stranger, Return of 150
Streatham Common 94
Sumner, Charles 57
Sunset Express 137
Sunshine Desserts 153
Surbiton 17, 50, 51, 135, 152
Surrey 154
Survivors 151
Sweeney, The 151
Sydney 66
Szlumper, W 110

Tardis 141
Tartar locomotive 12, 19
Tattoo parlour 114
Taxi! 151
tearoom 120
Teddington 51
telephones
    boxes 120, 140
    exchange 152, 153
    telephone room 48
television 122–123
Tennant, Neil 155
*Terminus (Television
    series)* 152
Terminus 133, 150, 151
Thames Embankment 85
Thatcher, Margaret 143, 146
Thompson, Derek 150
Thorndike, Dame Sybil 112
Three Men in a Boat 50, 154
Ticket Machine 135, 140
Tinworth Street 29
Titanic, RMS 108–109
Tite, William 15, 16, 24, 27
toll gate 21, 24, 42
toll house 129
Topolski, Feliks 153
Tower Hamlets Cemetery 53
Tower of London 134
Trafalgar, battle of 8
Trafalgar Square 26, 81
Trainspotting 31
Travolator 95, 98
Treaty of Canterbury 143
Troop train 77, 154
Troops 111, 124
Trotter, Derek 150
Tubbs, Cyril Bazett 66
turtle soup 10, 45
Twickenham Stadium 130
Tyler, Captain 73

Underground 152
uniform 17, 50

Union Jack Club 104, 114, 125
Union Street 76, 87
Upper Marsh 43

V1 127
V2 127
Vauxhall
    extension to Waterloo 28
    line to Kingston 15
    Necropolis Railway 63
    Nine Elms site 11
    origin of name 14
    Pleasure Gardens 14, 15
    Vauxhall Bridge 15
VE Day 128
viaduct 22, 23, 24, 27, 28, 29, 71,
    77, 81, 87, 105, 115
Victoria station 38, 142
Victoria Theatre 32
Victory Arch 117–118, 130, 144,
    150, 152
Village, The 116
Vilmouth, Jean-Luc 146
Vindaloo 155
Vine Street 27, 32, 35, 45, 83

W. Armstrong & Co 47, 95
Walker, Herbert 151
Walker, Johnnie 150
Walm Lane 113
Walton 18, 19
Wandsworth 11, 15, 22
Wandsworth High Street 40
Wandsworth station 17, 21, 23
War of the Worlds 75, 154
Warren, Captain Daniel 49
Warwick Gardens 146
Waterloo & City Railway
    (overground) 87
Waterloo & Royal Exchange
    Railway 87
Waterloo & Whitehall
    Railway 83
Waterloo Air Terminal 131
Waterloo Bridge 24, 27, 31, 42,
    43, 44, 58
*Waterloo Bridge Handicap,
    The* 32
Waterloo Bridge Road 32,
    103, 89
Waterloo clock 7, 112, 118,
    135, 150
Waterloo station cinema
    121–122
Welles, Orson 122
Wells, H.G 75, 154
Welsh Tourist Board 137
Wembley 114
West Brompton 142, 143
West End Girls 155

West End of London & Crystal
    Palace Railway 38
West Indies 45, 143
West London BEA Terminal
    132
West London Railway 75
West Norwood Cemetery 54
West Sussex 8
Westland S55 Helicopter 132
Westminster Aquarium 45
Westminster Bridge Road 27,
    28, 31, 34, 63, 66, 67, 68,
    98, 101, 105, 106, 107, 114,
    117, 127
Westminster Hall 134
Wey & Arun Canal 8
Weybridge 10
Weybridge station 18
Wheatstone, Charles 18
Whiffen, Charles Edward 117
Whitehall 82, 83, 86, 113, 134
Wimbledon 17, 21, 24, 41, 51,
    52, 116
Winchester 104
Winchfield 18
Windmill Pier 15
Windrush Generation 7, 133,
    134, 152
Windsor 41, 42, 45, 49, 37, 73,
    75, 143
Wisbey, Tommy 139
Wisdom, Norman 150
Witney, John 29
Woking 12, 17, 19, 24, 54, 66, 67
Woking Common 11, 17, 18,
    19, 56
Woking Railway Hotel 54
Woking signal box 18
Wooden Railway (Prosser's
    System) 24
Woodington, William
    Frederick 129
Woolwich 92
Woolwich ferry 89
Works locomotive 75S 92
World Cup 155
Wormwood Scrubs 144
Wrecker, The 152
Wrong Box, The 154
Yeovil 16, 132
YMCA 112, 125
York Road 24, 26, 27, 52, 38, 40,
    45, 44, 46, 71, 72, 80, 85, 86,
    94, 97, 101, 106, 107, 114,
    127, 130, 154, 138, 148, 151
Young, Francis 80

Zeppelin airship 114
Zola, Emile 130